Friends of the Earth
The real food book

real food
time to choose

FRIENDS *of the*
earth
for the planet for people

Thanks for help writing this book >>

Nicola Baird, Adrian Bebb, Simon Bernstein, Mike Childs, Sarah Finch, Ronnie Hall, Carol Kearney, Tony Juniper, Duncan McLaren, Andy Neather, Matt Phillips, Pete Riley, Peter Roderick, Liana Stupples, Mike Walton and Adeela Warley.

Design > Brenda Lardner
Photography > Peter Dazeley

ISBN 1 85750 328 7

Friends of the Earth works to protect and improve the conditions for life on Earth, now and for the future.

Friends of the Earth 26–28 Underwood Street, London N1 7JQ

Tel: 0171 490 1555
Fax: 0171 490 0881
E-mail: info@foe.co.uk
Website: www.foe.co.uk

Contents

 # Foreword

Thanks to a decade of headlines concerning food scares, environmental scandals and the crisis in farming, it hardly needs restating that there is something grievously wrong with the way most of our food is produced. Damage is being done to the land and to our health, and the animals we use for food are suffering unnecessarily.

Sometimes it can seem so hard for us consumers to pick our way through the food market place with a clean conscience that we may be tempted to give up altogether. That would be fatal. There are now enough of us who really care about the quality of our food and the way it is produced to make a real difference. There are also enough farmers, of livestock, grain, fruit and vegetables, who reject industrial farming practises in favour of good husbandry and sustainable agriculture, to offer real hope. I know dozens of farmers in Dorset alone who are dedicated to reducing or eliminating the use of unnecessary chemicals, and improving the quality of life of their livestock. Despite their minority status in the farming community they are not down hearted but optimistic; they feel that, finally, things may be moving their way. Why? Because they sense the growing support of a community which can taste the difference, and appreciate their efforts.

Though the term "real food" has been much bandied about in recent years I believe that, as applied alongside the campaigning vigilance that we have come to expect from Friends of the Earth, it can have "real meaning". This highly readable book performs two vital functions. By carefully exposing and explaining the abuses of industrial farming practises, it presents a compelling case for a consumer fight back. Then it goes on to explain what we can actually do to help - how to find and choose "real food" - food that is produced without the abuse of land, animals, people, or consumer trust. Food that tastes better, because it is better.

Hugh Fearnley-Whittingstall, River Cottage, Dorset

 **Introduction**

Why real food? >>

One of the most popular daytime TV shows is *Supermarket Sweep*. The show's concept is simple: contestants race around a supermarket stuffing their trolleys with goods until the clock is stopped. *Supermarket Sweep* may make a virtue out of naked greed, but it is also a telling satire of our nation's shopping habits. They are driven by quantity, not quality.

Pile goods high and give shoppers the illusion they are cheap has long been the mantra of the supermarket giants, and it's one that we have all fallen for. It's easy to feel there is plenty of choice in the supermarket. Wheeling a trolley slowly down the aisles past 50 different sorts of cereals, endless brands of tinned tomatoes and chiller cabinets filled with mild, medium and strong-flavoured cheddar gives most shoppers the feeling that they have more choice than they need. As you agonise between what to heat and eat for dinner tonight – perhaps chicken korma or lasagne – it is hard to believe that the modern system of farming and processing actually leaves shoppers with surprisingly little choice.

And it's not a healthy choice either. If it was up to you, no doubt you would choose food that was fresh and did you no long-term harm. You would not choose food contaminated with pesticide residues or filled with additives to ensure a long shelf life. Nor would you choose food produced in a way that paid farmers to apply these chemicals, and penalised against those who wanted to keep chemicals off their crops.

Yet every time you tuck into a ready-made meal that's exactly what you are choosing.

It's true that supermarkets stock hundreds of thousands of product lines, but if you want to eat food that is as unprocessed as possible the choice shrinks. It is obvious why: transforming raw products into ready-made meals has huge financial benefits for the manufacturers. They can charge much more for an apple pie than they can for an apple. A manufacturer needs to ensure that their pie is the choice of shoppers: they will wrap it in layers of bright packaging, boasting that it tastes "home made" to attract more customers; they may well add anti-oxidants and stabilisers to ensure it has a long shelf life. They can then sell the pie for many times the price of the humble apple.

You might think that a tart apple layer encased in pastry is quintessentially English. But you would be wrong. Few food manufacturers source locally – unless the product is cheaper. So the apples may come from the USA, the flour used to make the pastry case may have come from Canada. The sprinkling of sugar is from South America. To ensure the largest possible financial return the crops will have been repeatedly treated with chemicals that wipe out wildlife and may threaten the health of the workers who tend the crops. Taste will have been sacrificed for size. There may be pesticide residues.

Huge amounts of fuel and packaging will have been used to ship the apples around the world as they are transformed from crop into purée and finally pie. Their journey doesn't stop there – they will then be brought to a central depot in the UK before being trucked out to the point of sale store, before being driven home by a customer. Every new destination adds to the problem of climate change. Every layer of packaging has to be thrown away in already over-filled rubbish dumps.

This support for global, intensive farming whatever the environmental costs has led to dramatic changes in farming, shopping and the landscape.

For those people with enough time to worry about how healthy or sustainable this modern way of processing and eating is, there is very little information available. Product labels show everything – but nothing important. And they often do it in text which is so tiny it is a struggle to read, even under the bright lights of the dessert aisle. The label on your apple pie does not legally have to identify the country of origin - let alone the county where it was baked. Labels do not have to contain information about whether the product is free of genetically modified ingredients (more about this in Chapter 3). Labels never warn that this apple pie may contain toxic pesticide residues unless it is organically produced. Labels do not show the total amount of miles the ingredients have travelled to make the pie, or reveal the wildlife and biodiversity destroyed in its making. If they did many of us would get a nasty shock – surely the dinner shouldn't be better travelled than the diner?

The distance our food travels, and the amount of chemicals used to produce it, are fundamental to sustainable development. Food that is produced in a sustainable way is food which is produced without compromising the ability of future generations to meet their own food and water needs. It is produced in a way that does not trash the planet's resources unnecessarily. Sustainably produced food is farmed in a way which is beneficial to wildlife and the environment.

Yet the typical shopper, piling their supermarket trolley high with over-processed, over-packaged, over-travelled goods during the weekly shop, is buying into a system which is not sustainable. It is bad for our health and it is bad for the planet.

It's also an agricultural trend which is crippling the livelihoods of British farmers and local food producers. Most have no choice but to fit in with the demands of the multinational companies which control the way our food is farmed and processed - even if many do not want to do so.

"Although it may be easy for a farmer to grow a crop of organic wheat and convert it into flour, it can be prohibitively expensive to do so," explains Pete Riley, Food Campaigner at Friends of the Earth. "For example, the nearest mill to a Lincolnshire farm might be 40 miles away and be controlled by a large company. The farmer can get his crop milled, but the company will charge extra to keep the wheat separate so the farmer can sell it as locally grown and locally manufactured flour. So the consumer pays more for local-produced food!"

But we can do something about this. That's why Friends of the Earth (FOE) is running a Real Food Campaign. It's a campaign which enables you to use your purse power to choose real, tasty food farmed in a way that's good for the planet. It helps you use your power of persuasion to make the government support local farmers and locally-based food processing.

The Real Food Campaign is one that could be good for everybody. Friends of the Earth is not telling anyone what to eat. Instead we are asking why certain groups – government, multinationals, supermarkets and intensive farms – are preventing us from having fresh, tasty, safe food. This is a campaign about getting hold of the food you would eat if given the choice.

It's also a way of ensuring food is more fairly distributed. This is one of the key reasons why 800 million people on the planet do not have enough food to meet their basic nutritional needs.

Shoppers know that something is not quite right with the food we are currently being offered. Fears about genetically modified organisms and ingredients (shortened to GM or GMOs in this book) in our food have made us all more alert to the potential dangers that are lurking in our shopping baskets. Recent opinion polls have shown that three-quarters of the population do not want to eat GM food. That's why the Real Food Campaign is calling for producers to make their food safe, at the same time as finding ways to enable local producers to keep on making the delicious regional specialities – like Highland shortbread, Whitby kippers, Wensleydale cheese, Welsh lamb, Bakewell tart or Devon clotted cream – which make British cuisine distinctive.

In the first part of this book we track the reasons why the modern system of farming has made it normal to buy overly processed goods in supermarkets with little regard to season, environmental sustainability, health or local livelihoods. We explain why this is bad for local produce, farmers and for shoppers.

In the second section of the book you can find out about the many different ways of filling your shopping basket with real food. It may mean learning to scrub your vegetables clean and sometimes avoiding supermarkets. But as a result you will know that what you have chosen to eat is tasty or healthy (more often than not, both tasty and healthy) and is helping preserve local specialities.

As you will see, there are lots of ways you can get hold of safe, tasty food. You can help make the Real Food Campaign a success by following our six tips for choosing real food that is better for your health - and better for the planet. Surely that's too tempting a combination to resist?

What you can do >>
Six ways you can choose real food today

1   Avoid GM foods >

Before being imported to the UK, GM crops are often mixed together with normal ones. This makes it extremely difficult to label GM food accurately. Many foods that contain GM material such as soya oil and lecithin, do not have to be labelled at all. So: check for labels but beware, they can be confusing. Use our Good Label Guide (see Chapter 8).

The best option is to ask the supermarket manager which products contain GM ingredients, as each supermarket has a slightly different policy (see Chapter 8).

2   Buy local organic foods >

Locally grown produce from certified organic farms does not use pesticides, antibiotics, hormones, or genetically modified ingredients.

>> Find out if there is a delivery scheme near you (see Chapter 6).

>> Ask your supermarket and local shops to stock more locallym produced organic foods.

>> Get to know the labels (see our Good Label Guide in Chapter 8).

3 Buy fair trade products >

Fair trade means paying the producers a decent price for their products. Buying fairly traded products, such as coffee, gives support to communities which are looking after their environment. Fair trade, puts money back into local communities to give everyone a better standard of life. Fair trade allows real, lasting change and transforms people's lives.

4. Shop local >

Liberate yourself from the weekly supermarket trawl and sample your local shops and local produce. You'll have more say about who provides you with food and generally speaking the shorter the distance your food has travelled, the less pollution and wasteful packaging it requires. Similarly, importing food squeezes out local producers and creates a demand for unseasonal foods.

5 Buy direct >

Buying food direct from UK farmers and producers gives you fresh, seasonal produce and puts more of the profit into the farmers' hand.

>> Make use of farm shops if you have one near you.

>> Visit a local farmers' market, they're just like a street market except it is farmers selling their produce direct to consumers.

>> Find out about your local vegetable delivery schemes and other home delivery services in your area, some can even offer on-line e-mail ordering.

6 Grow your own >

Grow vegetables and herbs in your own garden, allotment or window box. It's a fun way of guaranteeing yourself fresh food, grown organically, and without clocking up any food miles.

Section A

Food fears: why worry about what you eat?

Chapter 1

Intensive agriculture:
a thoroughly modern mess >>

Tradition has it that farmers are champion moaners. The weather is never right; fuel prices are going up and profits are down. But when Somerset farmer Graham Bigwood's 10 calves sold for £2.97 at Taunton market in June 1999, it seemed that some farmers had reasons to beef. Each calf was selling for 29p - less than the price of a bottle of milk.

Back in October 1998 it was the turn of sheep farmers to face up to bankruptcy after sheep prices dropped to 25p an animal - less than a packet of crisps. Desperate farmers in Wales and Cornwall tried to cope with the crisis by dumping sheep they couldn't afford to feed, and couldn't afford to transport to market to sell, at RSPCA centres. Few farmers are immune, as the National Farmers Union's (NFU) rural summit research revealed recently. Farm incomes have fallen by a staggering 75 per cent over the past two years and are still falling – albeit from a peak in the early 1990s.

While the smaller farms struggle, many shoppers can be forgiven for not having noticed. The aisles are crammed with different products and the supermarkets run innumerable special offers. Basics like bread and tinned baked beans are practically given away in some stores. No wonder we feel confident enough about our food supplies that £18 million of food is wasted in the UK each week.

Farmers claim the problem is the strength of sterling. Sterling has hit its highest level since the early 1990s, which encourages supermarkets, food processing companies and caterers to buy cheaper imports rather than British products. But is it appropriate for the public to have sympathy for farmers who have fed their livestock on the remains of other animals? Who have ploughed up meadows and other important wildlife habitats and plastered their land with chemicals for years, all aided by huge subsidies from the taxpayer?

Surprisingly, the answer is probably yes: the thoroughly modern mess farmers find themselves in is not entirely their own fault. Farmers have been seduced by subsidies to destroy the countryside and have been locked into chemical use by agrochemical companies.

We can do something about the crisis in farming if we choose to do so – as much by campaigning as by making more informed shopping choices. But first let's look at the inherent problems with modern intensive farming to see why things have to change. We want a sustainable agricultural industry that gives shoppers the chance to buy healthy, tasty food and a fair deal for Britain's small farmers and specialist food producers.

Intensive farming >

Modern intensive farming is driven by the principle that more – and cheaper – is better. Modern produce is grown to be uniform in size and colour. There are premiums for out-of-season supplies – regardless of the environmental cost. Quality and sustainability have been ignored. Maximising production and reducing costs by replacing people with machinery and chemicals is a gamble that has paid dividends for some, but one that has also forced many people out of farming.

Fifty years ago, farmers used few artificial fertilisers and pesticides and many farms managed livestock and arable crops. Overall the impact of farming and food production on the environment was relatively benign, although yields and profits were lower. The problem was that after World War II food rationing, policy makers decided Britain should never again be in a situation where it could not feed itself – a view common in Europe.

Shoppers are still getting the legacy of post-war thinking – quantity and all-year-round availability whatever the environmental cost. But the result of the UK government's food policy, supporting intensive agriculture no matter what the environmental and social costs, has led to a dramatic change in farming, shopping and the landscape. It has also led to the rise of much more efficient production (at least for agribusiness) and more competitive retailing. But it has come with a cost. Now the thinking needs to change. What shoppers need is food that is safe, nutritious, tasty and affordable, and for it to be produced in a way which does not damage the environment.

Anyone for carrots? >>

Although British farmers are growing more carrots than ever before, the amount of land used for carrot growing in Essex, Norfolk, Suffolk, Lincolnshire and Nottinghamshire has remained unchanged. The incredible increase in yields, which allows five kilos of carrots to grow from just one square metre of land, is due to the liberal use of fertilisers and pesticides. But the build-up of pesticides has become so bad that since 1995 the Government has advised that carrots should be peeled and topped before eating to try and remove the chemical residues.

The only way that the costs of modern agriculture and food processing can be kept down is by 'externalising' them. This is when the true costs of growing a product are kept out of the chain of costs passed down from producers to consumers and reflected in the price tag of a product.

For example, heavy pesticide use means that yields of many vegetables have increased dramatically, reducing their production cost and price to shoppers. But there are costs associated with pesticides – for example, cleaning up drinking water supplies contaminated by them, or in the cost to the NHS of treating illnesses caused by them – which are not reflected in the price of vegetables on the supermarket shelf. We still eventually pay those costs, as taxpayers and in other ways. The BSE crisis has so far cost around £4 billion – or £155 for each UK taxpayer. In 1997 around 25,200,000kg of synthetic chemical pesticides were sold in the UK, yet each kilogramme of pesticide applied by farmers cost £7.57 to clean up. Everyone pays for this in their water bills. And other externalised costs cannot be quantified – for example the loss of traditional landscapes, and wildlife such as sparrows and brown hares.

This catalogue of problems could have been stopped years ago. Instead it has been maintained by the vested interests of governments in the UK and Europe, lobbied by agrochemical multinationals. It has also been reinforced by the EU's Common Agricultural Policy (CAP), which has encouraged intensive, chemical farming at the expense of wildlife and habitats.

Deadly cocktail >

Intensification in crop production means using large quantities of fertilisers and pesticides, including herbicides (also known as weedkillers), insecticides and fungicides. There are more than 300 chemicals approved for use on crops in the UK, and the UK's farmers spray around one billion gallons of them each year. Cox's apples grown in the UK, for example, get an average of 35 pesticide treatments before arriving at the supermarket.

The problem is that pesticides are harmful to human health as well as to the weeds, insects and funguses they are aimed at eliminating. Despite official limits on the permitted amount of pesticide residues allowed in food, these levels are regularly exceeded.

Possibly the most harmful toxins are the organophosphates (OPs) and organochlorines (OCs), a family of insecticides used against a wide range of crop and animal parasites and pests. OPs were originally designed as a poisonous nerve gas for warfare. OPs and OCs are toxic to all animals, including humans, and their effects on human health include mental and nervous disorders and a possible link to chronic fatigue syndrome.

Pesticides can affect us directly if we work with them or if they are blown towards us by wind. There are many such cases reported in the UK every year, often causing severe skin and eye irritation, and many more probably go unreported as people do not link the symptoms they suffer with contact from pesticides. But they get into our bodies mainly because they do not disappear after being sprayed: they stay on the skins of fruit and vegetables or are absorbed into them. Either way, they end up in our food – including processed food made from fruit and vegetables. Forty per cent of fresh produce contains pesticide residues, and it has been estimated that the average British diet contains residues of around 30 different pesticides.

We're all guinea pigs now >>

Government figures show that in 1998 half of all imported winter lettuce and 80 per cent of UK-produced winter lettuce contained pesticide residues; one in eight of the UK lettuces had residues over the Government's maximum residue level. Apples and nectarines have been found with pesticide residues 20 times the legal limit. More worrying still, Friends of the Earth research has shown that over a third of UK baby food contains pesticide residues 10 times that of EU limits. This is a particularly risky experiment as babies consume much more food in proportion to their body weight than adults.

Many pesticides are "persistent", which means they can stay in the soil for years after they were first applied, posing a continuing threat to human health and to biodiversity. For example, lindane, an organochloride pesticide related to DDT, has been banned or heavily restricted in many countries because of being repeatedly linked to breast cancer. Shocking research by health experts recently showed that more than 350 toxic chemicals, including lindane, can be found in breast milk.

Despite all this, lindane has not been banned in the UK. Each year around 80 tonnes of this deadly insecticide is sprayed on crops. Ministry of Agriculture studies have shown lindane residues in a range of British vegetables, grains, meat, dairy products, baby formula and animal feed. In 1996, for example, over a third of

Chemical Christmas >>

Surprises aren't always nice at Christmas, especially when they are part of the traditional Christmas menu. But in 1997 FOE revealed that most people were downing a chemical cocktail of pesticides and antibiotics during the Christmas dinner they had spent so long preparing. The toxic festive fare included:

Turkey - given antibiotic feed additives, to reduce the chance of disease spreading in cramped broiler sheds and as a growth promoter

Mashed potato - more than half of all UK spuds sold through shops may contain pesticide residues, including chlorpropham (weedkiller), thiabendazole (a systemic fungicide), and tecnazene (fungicide and sprout suppressant)

Carrots - can contain organophosphate insecticide

Sprouts - can contain dithiocarbamate fungicides and lindane

Xmas pud - even this may not be free of unwanted additives - brandy butter and chocolate may contain lindane, while nuts may contain methyl bromide.

British cow's milk was contaminated with lindane. In Lincolnshire, where lindane is used extensively, especially on sugar beet, breast cancer levels are 40 per cent above the national average.

Lindane and many similar chemicals build up in our bodies over many years, especially in our fat. It is also suspected of having disruptive effects on our hormonal systems. In addition, the cocktail effect of consuming a mixture of residues is unknown.

Fifty years on from the start of the revolution in agrochemicals, many farmers continue to believe they can't survive economically without applying chemicals. But pesticides and chemical fertilisers damage the environment. They wash out into nearby streams and rivers, contaminating the water. Nitrates, one of the main components of commercial fertilisers, pollute drinking water in this way. Up to four per cent of pesticides end up in water, and the cost of cleaning up this pollution is around £1 billion a year. Sheep dip is another problem: the powerful pesticides used on sheep to prevent parasites such as blow-fly and scab leak into groundwater and water courses.

Pesticides also destroy wildlife habitats on land, with severe damage to populations of birds and other wildlife. They have a serious impact on many 'arable weeds', which are now highly threatened, in turn wiping out seed-eating and insect-eating wild birds such as skylarks, thrushes, and mammals such as dormice.

Nature fights back >

The irony is that the more pesticides are used, the more that insects and parasites build up resistance – which farmers deal with by applying larger quantities of ever more deadly pesticides. For example, in the USA, around the start of the chemicals revolution in 1950 there were less than 20 insect species with a known resistance to chemical pesticides; by 1990 there were more than 500. This is in part because intensified farming causes similar parasite problems in crops as in animals: a 20-acre field planted with nothing but carrots, for example, attracts far worse infestations of carrot fly than would smaller-scale plots. Also, intensive breeding can make crops more prone to illness - for example apples selected for yield are more susceptible to certain diseases.

Chemical agriculture doesn't just damage the environment and human health: it produces inferior food. We are all familiar with watery tomatoes and tasteless apples. Chemical agriculture is the first step in a food chain which operates at every step on the principle that quantity – more tonnes of bigger tomatoes – is more important than quality or flavour. Indeed government statistics recently revealed that the nutritiousness of crops has actually declined as pesticide and fertiliser use has increased.

Animal farm >

Intensive farming means farming as many animals as cheaply as possible.

The suffering of battery hens, de-beaked and crammed into cages, has been well publicised, as has the now-outlawed practice of raising veal calves in crates. Yet although sales of "free range" eggs have risen, 85 per cent of eggs purchased in Britain still come from battery farms. Meanwhile, broiler chickens (raised for eating) are kept in sheds holding tens of thousands of birds, packed without room to move and sickly from stress, lack of exercise, ulcerated feet and other ailments. Turkeys are raised in similar conditions. They have been bred to have such an unnatural amount of breast meat that they are incapable of either mating or flying, and have to be artificially inseminated in unpleasant conditions. Pigs kept indoors in intensive conditions suffer from overcrowding, disease and distress, while those kept outdoors can suffer because they are bred to be lean.

Keeping large numbers of animals in cramped conditions makes them far more prey to diseases and parasites. To tackle these, animals are routinely treated with various medicines, notably antibiotics, usually mixed in with their feed or water. Antibiotics are also used as growth promoters to boost animals' weight-gain.

Almost all poultry, 80 per cent of pigs and nearly half of all sheep and cattle raised in the UK are routinely treated in this way. A 1998 Soil Association report found that farm use of tetracycline, an important antibiotic widely used in human medicine, has increased 15-fold in the past 30 years.

The same abuse of chemicals is happening on fish farms. In Scotland, salmon farmers use de-lousing chemicals, including organophosphates such as Dichlorvos, to treat their salmon for chronic infections of sea lice. In the wild, sea lice are a relatively insignificant parasite. They only become a problem when salmon are kept crowded into underwater cages in unnaturally large numbers – as many as 50 fish in a cubic metre of water.

More antibiotics are now fed to UK farm animals than to British people. Yet there is increasing evidence that this has harmful effects on the humans who eat the resulting meat; residues of tetracycline have been found in some British turkey and pork. The House of Lords Select Committee on Science and Technology concluded in a 1998 report that "there is a continuing threat to human health from imprudent use of antibiotics in animals" because antibiotic residues in meat are thought to lead to resistance to antibiotics in humans, rendering the drugs ineffective in fighting human illnesses.

It makes you sick >

Meat and eggs produced in these ways can transfer illnesses to humans via "pathogenic" bacteria. The bacterial agents salmonella and campylobacter, for example, are both endemic on intensive chicken farms. They spread between chickens because both laying and broiler chickens are fed food pellets that can contain the mashed-up waste meat and blood from poultry slaughter and meat scraps from catering waste. Some estimates put the amount of chicken on sale in the UK contaminated with either salmonella or campylobacter or both at around 60 per cent; recent tests by Sainsbury's suggested salmonella infections of up to 20 per cent in its chicken.

Far more dangerous is E. coli 0157, a bacteria that is passed to humans from the gut of cattle. The notorious 1996 outbreak in Lanarkshire, spread by meat pies, killed 26 people. While death is uncommon, the bacteria can cause great pain as well as permanent kidney and circulatory damage.

In total, reported cases of food poisoning have increased seven-fold since the early 1980s, to over 100,000 cases a year. This is probably a small proportion of the real total. Recent estimates put the annual figure as high as one million. The total cost of intestinal disease to the NHS is £750 million a year.

The most notorious case of disease transmitted by intensively farmed animals is of course BSE (bovine spongiform encephalopathy, or "mad cow disease"). BSE developed in cattle which were fed a protein-based feed that included material from sheep infected with scrapie, a brain disease. It is thought to have jumped the species barrier first to cattle and then, as "new variant" CJD, to humans. Aside from the human cost of several dozen deaths to date from CJD, BSE has cost the British taxpayer at least £4 billion to date. BSE was the result of an intensive farming experiment taken without the appropriate degree of caution given that the health of millions of people was at risk. It went wrong – and serves as a terrible warning against the similarly cavalier attitude to the safety of GM crops shown today by the biotechnology companies and government.

Summing up >

As this catalogue of disasters shows, all is not well down on the farm. Small farmers like Graham Bigwood are broke, or have already sold up. And organisations set up to champion farmers, like the Ministry of Agriculture Food and Fisheries (MAFF) seem unable to accept the consequences of the drive to intensify production and increase yields. Unfortunately this bias towards intensive farming is going to keep on forcing farmers into the chemical trap with dire consequences to the health of people and the planet.

This bias also explains MAFF's persistent refusal to accept that organic farming – a way of farming which is sustainable and practically chemical free – is suitable for anything other than a niche market. As a result the very few farmers which have managed to drop the chemicals and go organic, with all the resulting benefits for consumers and the wildlife on their land, have had minimal financial support. This can make life very tough for them, especially during the few years when their land is in conversion to an organic farm. The reasons why it is not just UK farmers who feel financially wedded to these unsustainable methods of farming are explained in the next chapter.

What you can do >>

See six ways you can choose real food today, page 11.

Chapter 2

Peaceful as the grave: our modern countryside >>

At the tiny village of Longcot in South West Oxfordshire things are not what they used to be. Here Jean Saunders, 53, has been collecting information for a Parish Conservation Plan and she is shocked by her findings. "I've been walking round all the fields in the parish looking for wildlife and recording anything of interest," explains Jean. "But it's been difficult. The wildlife has long gone. I've come to the conclusion that there's more life in my garden." It shouldn't be like this. Longcot is part of the countryside which inspired arts and crafts designer William Morris. Folk memory has it that spring is the time for cowslips and that the meadows are visited by curlews - but the reality is very different. "Where there has been no intensive farming, tiny areas which are either so wet that they haven't been drained or where farmers can't get their machinery, there are orchids and butterflies. But everywhere else it's really just an agricultural desert," complains Jean sadly.

It's a sorry story of a changing landscape which has been repeated throughout the UK because of the way policy makers in Europe say we should farm.

Britain's landscape has been subtly changed over thousands of years by settlement and agriculture. But while the pace of change was slow, wildlife could adapt, leaving traditional British farmscapes rich in plant and animal life.

Intensive agriculture has completely changed these rhythms. Agriculture is largely responsible for the loss of 95 per cent of our flower-rich meadows since 1945; for the loss of 80 per cent of lowland grasslands on chalk and limestone; and for the loss or significant damaging of almost a third of upland grasslands and heaths, and of half our coastal fens and marshes. Natural grassland is ploughed under, and modern methods allow deeper ploughing on steeper gradients than before. Grassland is over-grazed, encouraged especially by "headage" payments made to farmers by government and the EU.

Meanwhile, England's once abundant orchards are being grubbed up for EU payments – even as apple imports increase. Ponds and wetlands are drained: three-quarters of Britain's ponds have disappeared this century. Clearing trees, scrub and hedgerows causes soil erosion, a serious problem in parts of the UK. Ploughing steep land, winter crops, overgrazing, removal of hedgerows and trees and lack of attention to the soil's organic matter mean that 30 per cent of UK agricultural land is vulnerable to erosion. Once washed away, soil takes thousands of years to replace in some places.

This loss of habitat has had a disastrous effect not just on landscape but also on wildlife. Wild plants and flowers are killed by herbicides. This robs animals of their habitats. Birds that once fed on the seeds of plants at the fields' edge, or on the remains of crops in fields left fallow over the winter, are now faced with sprayed dead zones, and with winter feeding grounds planted with mono crops such as winter wheat or barley.

Britain lost over half its population of many once-common birds between 1975 and 1995. For farmland species like the skylark (down from more than four million to under two million) and song-thrush (population halved to around a million) intensive agriculture was the biggest culprit. For mammals too, intensive agriculture is a disaster. Brown hare numbers have dropped by around 80 per cent this century: it is virtually extinct in parts of England where meadows have been ploughed up.

The story doesn't have to have a depressing ending. Bird populations in many areas could probably recover if farming methods were changed. But once natural habitats such as the South Downs are gone, they are very difficult to recreate. The Downs took thousands of years of natural evolution and low-level sheep grazing to reach the sublime state they were in at the turn of this century; now they are being destroyed forever. The end result is that our landscape is becoming more lifeless, more uniform – and boring.

Where have all the birds gone? >>

"Skylark numbers have declined by three-quarters over the past 25 years. Since I started birdwatching as a teenager only one in four of the birds are left. It's all due to intensification of farming," explains Mark Avery, Director of Conservation at the Royal Society for the Protection of Birds (RSPB). "The RSPB doesn't blame farmers. But it does blame the Common Agricultural Policy. Things like the increased use of herbicides and the switch from hay to silage - so grass is cut earlier and is more heavily fertilised haven't helped." He pauses. "What else has knackered the skylark? Drainage so that wet squishy areas have been brought into production and the switch from planting cereal crops in the spring to the autumn, which means that the skylark cannot feed on weeds and seeds spilled in the stubble during the tough winter months." It's a gloomy list, and with good reason. "I can't think of anything that happens in the countryside which is good for the skylark. It's happened over such a short period of time and now this is a bird which could disappear. The skylark stands as a symbol of what happens to loads of birds, insects and plants - they are all getting a right hammering. No one wants this to happen, but it's built into the way farmers' farm."

In short, intensive farming greatly reduces "biodiversity" – the variety of life on our planet. In reducing biodiversity, we harm ourselves in many ways. We draw our scientific knowledge from the natural world, and when we exterminate species, we lessen the resources which will help us develop new protection from diseases and the like. Destroying biodiversity also undermines local economies and destroys unique and precious places.

The rural rot >

Highly mechanised chemical agriculture produces far more with far less work. Over the past ten years, around a third of the regular full-time farm worker jobs on UK farms have disappeared. The result is unemployment – now a chronic problem in many rural parts of Britain, as it is in regions practising intensive agriculture in Europe.

Some commentators play down the importance of job losses in farming because of the small size of the farming sector in the UK. It is true that only about two per cent of the UK workforce is employed in agriculture – less than 800,000 people in 1996. But in some regions the proportion is far higher – more than 10 per cent in South Devon, for example. The remaining jobs tend to be more casual or part-time, and less well paid.

And as farm jobs disappear, other parts of the rural economy – from equipment manufacturers to small shops to play groups – all suffer. A new set of problems appears: many rural areas have become depopulated, with fewer services for those that remain. People have to drive further to work, increasing congestion, energy consumption and pollution.

CAP uncovered >

The European Union's Common Agricultural Policy (CAP) has greatly encouraged the intensification of farming. Payments to farmers under the CAP are made largely on the basis of a given subsidy for a given area of a particular crop or numbers of livestock, or for not growing anything ("set-aside"). There are still also price supports for some products. Either way, the choice for farmers has been simple: produce as much as possible of the products with the highest CAP subsidies.

The introduction of this system in 1992 to replace the old one of guaranteed price supports has ended scandals such as the 1970s and '80s "butter mountain" and "milk lake". Yet farmers throughout the EU, including Britain, continue to make large sums of money by specialising in arable crops and by maximising their production as far as possible through mechanisation and chemical inputs. Mixed farming based on crop rotations to build fertility and control pests and diseases is long gone on most farms. Set-aside in the UK cost £215 million in 1995/96. And it has helped rich farmers far more than small ones: several British cereal farmers make over £1 million a year each in set-aside payments alone.

The CAP has had a damaging effect on the environment and rural economies. It has encouraged the use of agro-chemicals like fertilisers and pesticides. It has encouraged larger and larger farms using more mechanisation and less labour. By contrast it devotes minimal funds to the environment.

"There are historic reasons for subsidy of agriculture," explains Pete Riley, Food and Biotechnology campaigner at Friends of the Earth. "Britain was made vulnerable during World War II to U-boats knocking out grain being shipped from America and Canada. Before the war farming in the UK had been neglected. But once the decision was made to never risk food shortages again, things changed. This support was followed up by decisions by CAP to subsidise our farmers, made to protect farmers in Europe and maintain a viable agricultural industry – particularly against competition from North America where production costs are so much lower."

The consequence of this decision is that intensive farming, which causes so many environmental problems and has caused so much misery for smaller, mixed farms, is widespread across Europe. "Intensive farming produces a uniform product," adds Riley. "Farms are geared up to maximising production which is bad because it does not allow people who want to farm less intensively to do so on a level playing field." This means that small farm after small farm has gone out of business, only to be gobbled up by larger estates which are better at working the system. It has also led to an astonishing over-application of chemicals, mistreatment of animals and increasing concerns about the effect of this type of farming on people's health and on wildlife.

Half cut>>

Unbelievably Ian Hurst, who farms 800 acres on the East Yorkshire Wolds was fined more than £2,000 because he did not mow his set-aside by 15 August. "It was a wet year so a lot of pheasants and partridges were having a second brood, because they had lost the first. I could see they were nesting on the set-aside strips, so I decided to leave the mowing for a couple of weeks - otherwise it would have been carnage," says Hurst. But the inspectors from MAFF, following the CAP rule book, turned up two days after deadline and immediately issued a fine because he had not applied in writing for a mowing extension. "They could see a lot of young chicks, but the system is so bureaucratic. I felt the inspectors had zero understanding of set-aside objectives which is meant to be a positive environmental tool," adds Hurst. "Farming is getting scary. They wouldn't accept my reasons then. You find you are monitored from outer space. Inspectors turn up saying they can't match their satellite imagery with what we should be doing on the ground. It's just like Orwell's *Animal Farm*."

There is general agreement among European politicians that the CAP is too expensive: it costs £28 billion a year, or nearly half the total EU budget. In 1996/97 this cost the typical British family around £200. There is already large-scale fraud – well over a quarter of a billion pounds a year. It will become even more unworkable when Eastern European countries start to join the EU, with their large and more traditional farming sectors.

There are alternatives, such as those suggested by the European Commission's 1997 Agenda 2000 report. Many of the ideas in

Agenda 2000 seek to change farming. There is scope to give more support to labour- and knowledge-intensive systems including organic and mixed conventional farming. There is also a suggestion to cut crop subsidies, offsetting these cuts with "direct compensatory payments" if farmers meet certain environmental care requirements, and with subsidies that reward the benefits of more labour-intensive and diversified farms. However Agenda 2000 still does not address food quality. "It's more about facilitating the expansion of the EU into Eastern Europe keeping within the CAP budget and ensuring that EU farm support does not upset free trade agreements," explains Riley.

In order to help shoppers obtain real food, CAP has to change. It must support the communities that need it most, and promote jobs and local economic growth. In particular it should reward farmers who care for the environment, and not simply encourage higher and higher production regardless. Not only has the EU lacked the political will to do this, but it's big brother, the World Trade Organisation, is equally unlikely to put people and the environment first.

World trade rules>

The World Trade Organisation (WTO) is an intergovernmental body that was set up in 1995, to administer global rules governing international trade. However, the WTO's working brief is to promote free trade. In practice, this means that governments actually work within the WTO to develop international rules that can inhibit the use of regulation at the regional and national levels. Because the WTO is now the world's most powerful intergovernmental institution, it has been able to promote international trade at the expense of local and national trade. For example, the WTO's decision in July 1999 in favour of the USA and Canada over an EU ban on hormone-treated North American beef has meant that the US is implementing devastating sanctions on a wide range of European products from cheese to truffles, despite those industries having no connection to the hormone beef dispute.

Although agriculture is still heavily protected in many countries, including those in the European Union, the aim of some governments is to remove subsidies entirely. This could mean that subsidies which could be used for beneficial purposes, like protecting the rural environment and promoting rural employment, would stand no chance.

The WTO is also bad for European consumers who want to buy products produced in a particular way - fairly or sustainably, for example. Although WTO rules are a bit hazy on the subject, the general rule of thumb is that if it interferes with international trade it has to go. That's why the US was able to claim massive compensation from the EU in return for lost trade in bananas grown by American companies like Chiquita in Latin America. What consumers want isn't important in the global scheme of things. WTO rules are.

Fair deals >

There is also an equity issue: the UK food distribution and retailing system does little to help developing world farmers. Whether trading in the products that we cannot grow at home, such as coffee or cocoa, or in the ones we don't really need, like Zimbabwean mange-touts and Chilean apples, the terms of trade have always been strongly weighted against developing world producers. On average, for example, just 10 per cent of the price of bananas grown in the Caribbean goes to the growers. Most supermarkets and other industry players have done little to try to change this. What moves have been made towards "fair trade" – for instance in coffee – have been the initiatives of development and aid pressure groups and of specialist companies like Café Direct.

Even when the development of UK markets for farm products helps developing world producers kick-start industries, the kind of farming it encourages is often not sustainable. Much of it needs huge quantities of water, especially for raising animals, causing potential shortages and damage to thin tropical soils. Other types of export-based farming are even more damaging. Prawn farming in Thailand, Bangladesh and India has grown at a phenomenal rate during the 1990s, making money for a few agribusinessmen and bringing tiger prawns to the highest class restaurants and even humble pub kitchens throughout the UK. This dining trend has also resulted in the clearance of thousands of acres of mangrove swamp, damaging delicate ecosystems, increasing pollution and exacerbating local water shortages. And there is another problem. Cheap imports from overseas can threaten small domestic producers and UK jobs. That's why we need a switch from intensive farming to more sustainable approaches to help farmers and rural economies everywhere. But to do that, the rules of the WTO and CAP need to be changed.

Summing up >

Paradoxically, most British farmers have not done very well out of intensive agriculture. Small farmers have been steadily squeezed out by agribusiness, and those that remain are increasingly isolated by the demands of the supermarket chains and the vagaries of globalised agricultural commodity prices. Each crisis in farm prices is worse than the last; the present crisis is worse than that of the 1990-92 recession. NatWest bank predicted in late 1998 that up to 15 per cent of full-time farmers would go out of business. With figures like this, it is perhaps not surprising that one British farmer a week commits suicide.

What you can do >>
See six ways you can choose real food today, page 11.

Chapter 3

Frankenstein foods: the threat of GMOs >>

Not content with coaxing bigger and more crops from the soil, a small group of multinational agribusiness companies is now developing a whole new generation of crops. These are genetically modified or genetically engineered crops (often known as genetically modified organisms, or GMOs.) GMOs represent a potentially dangerous new frontier for the food production system – and for the environment and human health. Yet they are already on our supermarket shelves in the form of ingredients grown in the USA, and are close to being grown commercially in this country.

Genetic modification is very different from the kind of cross-breeding that has been practised for hundreds of years to produce fatter pigs or bigger carrots. It involves taking genes from a variety of completely different organisms and combining them to produce a plant with new qualities. In effect, scientists can choose certain genes from a given organism's DNA, the set of biological instructions imprinted on its cells, and insert them into the DNA of an unrelated organism. For instance, in an experiment researchers isolated a gene in the arctic flounder which prevents the fish from freezing in icy water, and transplanted it to tomatoes and strawberries to give them greater resistance to frost.

Most of the GM growing experiments conducted in the UK so far have been devoted to oilseed rape (an arable crop producing seeds which are used to produce cooking oil), sugar beet, fodder beet for animals, and maize. GM potatoes and wheat will be next. Many of the genetic modification experiments done so far have been aimed at producing plants with a resistance to a herbicide which they can then be sprayed with. For example, US-based multinational Monsanto has developed soybean and cotton plants that are resistant to its herbicide RoundUp. Another Monsanto product, the genetically modified hormone Bovine Somotropin (BSt), is in use in the USA, where it is injected into cows to encourage higher milk yields. For safety reasons BSt has been banned in the EU until the end of 1999.

Genetic engineering is a technology with potentially catastrophic consequences for the environment. Genes and their functions are still poorly understood, and the consequences of genetic engineering are unpredictable. GM food could release unpredictable toxins or allergy-causing substances into our food. Many GM foods contain genes which could confer resistance to commonly used antibiotics such as ampicillin. A 1994 report by the Government's advisory committee on GM foods warned that these could get passed on to bacteria in the gut of humans and animals, rendering medicines ineffective.

Frankenstein foods >>

One GM product was withdrawn from tests after a gene in it taken from the brazil nut triggered a nut allergy in people eating the product in tests. Research on BSt, which is used in some GM trials, has shown that it may increase a growth factor in the gut, suggesting a potential link to cancer. And in February 1999 the scandal over the suppression of the findings of food scientist Arpad Pusztai revealed that his experiments suggested that rats fed with GM potatoes showed a similar increase in gut size as well as damage to their internal organs, immune systems and brains.

The long-term effects on the environment could be catastrophic. There is a risk of genetic pollution of wild plants – for instance by cross pollination of GM oilseed rape with the already widely dispersed feral version of the plant and other wild relatives, such as wild turnip and wild radish. This could be especially damaging with

GM crops that are resistant to herbicides, potentially creating herbicide-resistant plants, already dubbed 'super-weeds'. Because genetic engineers are playing around with genes which give resistance to several different herbicides, there is a chance that weeds could be created with resistance to more than one product.

The companies and the UK Government insist that herbicide-resistant GM crops will help the environment by reducing the amount of herbicides that farmers need to spray. This claim is at best naïve. Farmers already know what happens if you over-use pesticides: pests develop resistance and become 'super pests'. Throughout the world, insects, fungi, weeds and parasites have quite rapidly developed resistance to thousands of products. Yet herbicide-resistant crops are provided with a ready-made gene with which they can pass on the trait to their wild relatives, without the need for evolution.

Understanding government's pet project >>

As health concerns about the the arrival of GMOs in so much of our food spread - soya is used in around 70 per cent of all ready-meals as well as margarine, chocolate, beer and baby food - people started asking why the Government was so intent on backing biotechnology. The answer could be simple: Labour is close to the biotech lobby. In June the *Daily Mail* calculated that officials at the Ministry of Agriculture had held 104 meetings with biotech companies since Labour took office back in May 1997 – the equivalent of one meeting a week. But the figure could be far higher once meetings with the Prime Minister and officials and ministers are added in.

Herbicide-resistant crops are designed to resist weedkillers, such as glyphosate and glufosinate. These products kill all plants in the field and field margins, except the crop, creating a sterile field. No weeds means no cover and food for insects and no food for birds or other wildlife.

Meddling with the building blocks of life is simply not well enough understood yet to start feeding ourselves the results. Despite this the GM revolution is well under way. The first clearly labelled GM food to appear in British supermarkets was tomato purée, but most simply sneaked into our favourite foods - even though GM crops cannot yet be commercially grown in the UK. This is because about a third of the 1998 US soya crop is genetically modified and has been mixed with the conventional soya crop. This makes it almost impossible for retailers to label food, and it is why GM soya has turned up in so many ready-made meals, from pies to pizzas, as well as ice cream, bread, margarine and baby food.

Over here

Since 1992 there have been more than 500 field tests of GMOs in the UK. Although many farmers are still reluctant to have a GM crop trial on their land, more than half claim they would want to grow the crops if they were released commercially.

GM crop products are also now appearing in UK animal feed. And despite the most recent wave of public concern over GM foods, the UK Government has backed the biotechnology companies developing GM technology. Full results of independent government research will not be available until 2001, by which time GM ingredients may be in many of the foods we buy.

In fact not all sections of the Government are as gung-ho about GM foods as Prime Minister Tony Blair. The Government attempted in 1998 to set up a scheme in which supermarket chains would pass on information gathered from their 'loyalty cards', which would enable government researchers to track the health of those who regularly bought GM products for potential allergies, cancer and

How government ended up in biotech's pocket >>

Why does Tony Blair seem more concerned about supporting the biotech industry than about protecting the environment and public health? The UK Government has actively encouraged GM trials in the UK and has persistently refused to sign up to a freeze on GM crops in Europe. It has ignored the warning from its Chief Scientific Adviser, Sir Robert May, who believes that GM crops could lead to further decline in song birds, insects, wild flowers and hedgerows. While consumers were saying they didn't want to eat GM foods, McDonald's was removing GMOs from its meals; supermarkets were trying to get GMOs out of their own brand foods and a number of British food firms announced that they were going GM free, the Government was trying to change the law to speed up the commercial development of GM crops. The problem for the Government is that it has already invested large sums in the new technology - £22 million during 1998 compared to a miserly £2 million on organic farming - and seems unable to admit that this is money badly spent. There is also the threat of World Trade Organisation penalties. One of the key reasons that the Government keeps on opposing the introduction of a ban in Europe on imports of GM foods and crops in the UK is because it claims it might face yet more trade penalties.

birth defects. Following the scheme's exposure by Friends of the Earth in January 1999, the supermarkets decided it wasn't such a good idea.

Among a clutch of multinationals including Novartis, Zeneca and AgrEvo, it is Monsanto that has led the GMO revolution. Before 1998, few people had heard of GMOs; that changed with the campaign run by FOE and other environmental groups from early 1998. By mid-1998, more than three out of four members of the public polled by MORI/Genewatch said that they didn't want GM crops grown in the UK until more research had been done. Once exposed, Monsanto mounted a £1 million-plus advertising campaign claiming that all it really wanted was debate. The series of seven different ads attracted more than 80 complaints to the industry watchdog, and eventually a reprimand from the Advertising Standards Authority.

But the campaign fell flat. By August MPs banned genetically engineered crops from restaurants and bars in the House of Commons because they did not meet the Palace of Westminster caterers' ethical and environmental criteria - even though the public was still expected to eat up their GMOs. So it was little surprise that by October almost 60 per cent of those questioned told Friends of the Earth/NOP that they didn't want supermarkets to sell GM foods. A leaked Monsanto report confirms that the company's PR campaign has failed badly to date, with public support "collapsing".

Feed the world?

Aside from the biotechnology companies' assurances about the safety of GM technology, they claim that GM products will help feed the world. This is nonsense. People starve in the developing world mostly because they have no money for food and no access to land – not because there is no food. What GM products will do is tie farmers in the developing world into even tighter control by Northern agribusiness, through strict patenting of all GM seeds and innovations such as plants with a "terminator" gene. Terminator technology makes any seed produced sterile, forcing farmers to buy new seed rather than save and plant their own as they have always done. These concerns have sparked widespread demonstrations.

Why Bob Shapiro wants to deny you choice >>

Robert Shapiro is Chief Executive Officer of the American multinational Monsanto which has been leading the race to put GE products on the market. He is a man who thinks of himself as a visionary, claiming gene technology will be a second Green Revolution. The only snag is that this one looks set to be just like the last: more about making bucks than feeding the world. Shapiro has tried to explain his ideas to the press, but they just don't add up. "The tension between the short-term and the long-term is one of the fundamental issues of business - and of life," he told the *Harvard Business Review*. But if Monsanto's RoundUp Ready soybeans, developed at least in part to boost sales of Roundup herbicide, turn out not to be safe for us or for the countryside, then his reassurances about corporate short-termism at the expense of long-term environmental safety will ring hollow indeed.

Farmers in North America, where the GM products of Monsanto and others are now well established, are experiencing similar problems to the Indian farmers. Unbelievably, Monsanto is suing Canadian and American farmers for "stealing" its seeds: the company has sent in private detectives to gather evidence from crops on the offenders' property, and set up a hotline for farmers to inform on neighbours who have "stolen" Monsanto GM seeds. Sued farmers claim that their plants have been accidentally pollinated by GM crops on neighbouring fields. In India, where thousands of peasant farmers, who rely on the practice of saving seed - a farming habit which biotech companies want to eliminate by tough licence agreements and 'terminator' technology - have attacked Monsanto offices.

Show us the label

The GM issue has been made more complicated by confusing labelling laws. For example most foods that contain GM material, such as soya oil, lecithin and GM enzymes, do not have to be labelled. Whilst the refusal of US growers to segregate GM from non-GM soya and maize means that it has become impossible for most retailers to guarantee whether products contain GM soya or not, even if they want to respond to consumer pressure.

Eating out >>

Foodies have been watching with growing alarm at the way GM ingredients are turning up in everything from blueberry muffins to sun-dried tomato bruschetta. That's why nearly all of the UK's top 23 restaurants - as listed in the influential *Good Food Guide 1999* - have added their weight to FOE's call for a five-year ban on GM foods and crops. It's not just the best restaurants that have acted though, even your local café now has to label food containing GM ingredients. The move came in an EU regulation and applies as much to the Savoy Grill as the chip van on the A34. However there are loopholes in this EU labelling law because some ingredients, like GM oil and lecithin, do not have to be labelled. Be warned: labels are not always clear. The only way to fight back is to ask.

New research from Friends of the Earth shows large areas of our countryside being turned into an open air genetic test site. The experiments - carried out by UK companies and multinational biotech corporations - raise the spectre of irretrievable genetic pollution of other crops and wild flowers.

FOE has analysed government approvals for genetic engineered test sites over the past five years, and has identified hundreds of test sites in the UK countryside. Most sites are testing crops that can withstand doses of weedkiller, in particular AgrEvo's Challenge and Monsanto's RoundUp. Although no genetically modified crops can be grown commercially in the UK, genetically engineered crops are widely grown on an experimental basis. Some test sites are vast, covering an area that could fit one hundred football pitches.

Public consultation on test sites has been virtually non-existent. Companies must put a notice in a local newspaper but no formal consultation takes place. No application has been turned down due to local opposition. But, as Adrian Bebb, Biotechnology Campaigner at Friends of the Earth, explains: "Genetic pollution is irretrievable and, unlike an oil spill, cannot be cleaned up. Once out in the environment these new organisms can replicate and reproduce. The long-term consequences of allowing so many test sites are unknown and frankly reckless given our present understanding of this technology. If your neighbour wants to build an extension you have the right to object and be heard. But when it comes to growing genetically engineered crops the public and farmers have no influence. Public consultation on this vital issue has been pitiful and meaningless."

Gloves off

You would think that one way to avoid GM foods is by eating organic products, which are not allowed to contain any GM ingredients. But even this guarantee could be compromised because the Government allows GM test sites near organic plots.

When Guy Watson moved his organic vegetable farm to picturesque Buckfastleigh he had high hopes of expanding his customer base so Riverford Farm organic vegetables was selling nationwide. But he never dreamt that his passion for organic veggies was going to bring him into a courtroom battle with one of the world's largest agro-chemical companies, Sharpes International Seeds, now taken over by Avanta.

Watson's family business secured organic status back in 1987; it now has 600 hectares, making it the largest independent producer of organic vegetables in the UK. Problems started when genetically modified (weedkiller-resistant) maize was planted on a neighbouring experimental farm the other side of the River Dart.

Watson wasn't the only one worried. The Soil Association, which verifies Riverford produce as genuinely organic-grown, warned that his sweetcorn would lose its organic certification if it was cross-pollinated by the GM maize because genetically engineered foods are forbidden under organic standards.

Before the courtroom drama began, Watson's lawyers, backed by FOE, the Soil Association and others, pleaded with Environment Minister Michael Meacher to save his organic status - and livelihood - by ordering the GM crop to be destroyed. Meacher refused. As a result Guy Watson called in the lawyers a couple of weeks before the GM maize was due to pollinate allowing maximum risk of contamination of his organic crop from cross pollination.

The Court of Appeal ruled that the Government acted unlawfully in allowing the genetic maize trial to go ahead. However, the judges refused the plea by Watson to have the trial crop removed.

As Pete Riley, Food Campaigner at Friends of the Earth, pointed out: "This demonstrates that rather than being tightly regulated, the rush to develop these Frankenstein foods has led to an astonishing government disregard towards even the most basic laws."

"The real issue is not so much the danger from this trial as the fact that it's the tip of the iceberg," warns Watson. "Once GM maize is on the national seed list, it'll be impossible to grow organic sweetcorn anywhere in the South of England."

By June 1999 his warning was reinforced by a shocking report commissioned by the MAFF from the John Innes Centre in Norwich. This concluded that it was already impossible to guarantee that foods now sold as GM-free, including organic fruit, vegetables and cereal, could remain completely uncontaminated by either GM pollen or seed. The key problem is that pollinating insects, like bees, do not operate no-fly zones. As a result more than 90 of Britain's 1000 organic farms may be at risk because they are sited within a six-mile radius of a GM test site.

Who's responsible? >>

Getting the law right may be just as important as getting the biotech science right. That's because it is not clear who will foot the bill if the biotech experiments go wrong. If this issue is not sorted out consumers, farmers, retailers and GM companies may be forced to fight out the issue in the courts – and already leading insurance companies and liability lawyers are concerned that GM companies and others could find it hard to obtain adequate cover against any claim for damages. At the end of June 1999, Friends of the Earth teamed up with Alan Simpson MP to try and get a bill through Parliament which will make the producers of GM food and crops liable for any health or environmental damage they may cause – unless they can show that they did all in their power to prevent it. To show how serious the issue could be, more than 200 directors of the 35 companies with consent to release GMOs, the chief executives and managing directors of the top 15 animal feed manufacturers, top 30 human food manufacturers and top 15 supermarkets, were sent a registered letter warning them about their potential personal liability.

Summing up

As with the rest of the intensive food production system, the real concern of the companies' involved in gene technology is not to improve human health or bring food to the hungry, it is to make profit for their relatively small group of shareholders. And they appear willing to do this without predicting the possible, devastating, environmental consequences on either people or the planet.

In just a couple of years Britain has become a vast genetic laboratory. This pollution of Britain has been brought about by greedy seed companies and a conciliatory government. Everyone should have the right to say "no" to genetically engineered food, but we will all be effected by this Frankenstein food experiment unless we make sure that its promoters start to listen to our demands. We may have to shout loud - even when scientists at English Nature, the Government's own statutory wildlife advisor, called for a three-year moratorium on the commercial growing of GM crops, which was quickly backed by more than 100 groups, including Christian Aid, Townswomen's Guilds and Action Aid, the Government ignored the call for caution.

Choosing biotechnology as a solution to the excessive use of chemicals which is destroying wildlife and affecting our health is ridiculous. GM crops are not the way forward for farming. Farming which uses a wide range of crops and fewer chemicals is not only better for the environment, but can also provide better food security for the world's poor.

Many farmers are more able to protect themselves against crop failures by using a range of different crops adapted to local conditions. In the UK there are much safer ways of reducing the amount of chemicals used in agriculture than by introducing GM crops. For example by working out when there is a weed problem, and only then applying chemicals, farmers can reduce their pesticide use by up to 97 per cent. The facts are clear. Sustainable, environmentally-friendly farming would be better for everyone's health.

What you can do >>

Find out more about GMOs on FOE's

award-winning website at www.foe.co.uk

Chapter 4

Off our trolleys: not so super markets >>

Although GM ingredients like soya and maize have been sneaked into the food chain in the USA with surprisingly little protest from American farmers or shoppers, people in Britain have real fears about serving Frankenstein foods. What they know is that the potential long-term effect of gene foods on people's health and the environment is not known, and that government research is not due out until 2001.

Yet gene foods were very nearly dished up without debate in the UK too. They came in bread, biscuits, baby food, ice-cream, ready meals and even beer. Until 1998 few shoppers realised that they were eating genetically modified ingredients whether they wanted to or not - and most didn't want to. But with the exception of Iceland, the supermarket chains claimed nothing could be done to remove - or even label - GM ingredients. How wrong shoppers have proved them.

Instead of accepting this news, shoppers told the big stores to think again. After an October 1998 survey showed that nearly 60 per cent of shoppers in the Midlands wanted stores to stop selling GM foods, Friends of the Earth took a new campaigning weapon on tour. This was the Gene Beast - part Frankenstein monster, part grotesque of GM vegetables - which helped warn shoppers that their local supermarket was stocking unlabelled GM foods.

For example, one cold November day the Gene Beast went shopping at two centrally-based Leicester branches of Sainsbury's. "The Gene Beast was brilliant at getting its picture in the local newspapers which really drew the public's attention to the issue of GM foods," said local campaigner Celia Barden, "and because councillors read local papers it helped get GM foods off the menu at local schools."

The Gene Beast took a day trip to France; it visited more than 100 stores nationwide; it attended the Supermarket of the Year awards to protest against the winner, Tesco's initial refusal to take GM products off the shelf and at Kingston Green Fair, in May 1999, joined an expert panel for a debate about GM foods. "It can be difficult getting people's attention at an outdoor event so we started with a gig," said musician Jerry Coates who organised the Gene Beast's Kingston visit, "including a rock version of an anti-GMO song and then we held a debate. The compere introduced an organic farmer, a Green Party representative, and MP Edward Davy and then our surprise industry guest, looking 'the picture of pure health, just one look can make you see how GM food is good for you,' and with that the revolting Gene Beast walked on, making everyone laugh."

On target >

FOE and the Gene Beast targeted supermarkets for very good reasons. These days when people ask for directions to the nearest shop, they are usually expecting to be shown the way to a supermarket, not a village grocer or bakery. The most obvious change in our eating and food buying habits in the UK over the past 25 years has been the places where we find that food. That's why just five supermarkets now account for nearly three-quarters of all grocery sales.

Supermarkets have revolutionised the way we buy food. They have made many more products available: the joys of croissant, sun-dried tomatoes and fresh yellow fin tuna are now available in much of the country. In effect supermarkets have created a demand for products that no one missed - who craved avocado 365 days a year before the supermarkets made it available?

The supermarkets run their own nationwide distribution systems, dictating products, quality and prices to a smaller and smaller number of large-scale farmers. Although a wide range of food and drink is on offer, much of it is imported including many items that could be grown in the UK such as apples and lettuce. These products are shipped in energy-intensive ways - for example, green beans are flown in from Kenya by air freight. As a result the average distance food is transported from field to plate has doubled over the past 20 years. It is a trend which has resulted in such energy-intensive methods of farming and transport that modern food uses more fossil-fuel energy in its production than it provides food energy.

Like our diet, the modern food system is highly processed. Once it leaves the farm, much of our food goes to factories for processing before arriving in our shops. In the past agricultural regions have often tried to add value to their products on the spot with relatively simple techniques, such as the canning of fresh fruit and vegetables. But nowadays far more money is to be made from the creation of new and more complex manufactured food products, like fish fingers, breakfast cereals, or margarine. Food processing companies make money by 'adding value' to basic food commodities. For example, a company can sell a given weight of fish for much more if it processes it as fish fingers than if it was simply sold on the slab.

This generally has a detrimental effect on the quality of the food we eat. As companies try to increase their profits, they generally reduce the quality of the raw ingredients that go into their food products. They cover up poor quality ingredients by over-processing them, adding various chemical preservatives, flavourings, colourings, sweeteners and salt.

Many of the ingredients in processed foods, particularly meat, carry a greater risk of disease and contamination. The BSE crisis revealed the use of "Mechanically Recovered Meat" (MRM) in some cheap frozen and other processed meat products. MRM is made by sucking all remaining scraps of meat and sinew from bones and carcasses, producing a kind of meat slurry that needs to have a lot added to it to make it palatable. Little better is "re-formed meat", a mixture of low-grade off-cuts and additives that is formed into products like "meat roll" and a variety of anonymous chicken products such as nuggets.

This trend to more and more processing and liberal use of additives has led to major changes in our diet, whether we want them or not. A whole range of unhealthy products has been mass-marketed, changing public tastes. The typical Western diet now contains more fatty, salty, sugary foods and less fresh fruit, vegetables and unprocessed grains and pulses.

Convenience foods, which are mostly heavily processed and now also probably contain GMOs, represent around a third of the average British family's food bill. Despite years of food experts advising us of the benefits of a Mediterranean-style diet – more fresh fruit and vegetables, less sugar, salt, fat and animal products – the UK, with Finland, still suffers Europe's highest rates of heart

Buying rubbish >>

Cereal buyers are getting a lot less than they bargain for thanks to the unnecessary packaging so beloved of supermarkets, one survey revealed in 1998. Cereal packets are so unnecessarily large that they contain up to 60 per cent air, and only 40 per cent cereal. Friends of the Earth slammed supermarkets and manufacturers for wasting thousands of tonnes of paper on useless packaging. The survey, by Staffordshire County Council Trading Standards Office, looked at 133 breakfast cereal products. The worst offender was Sainsbury's - who claimed in an annual Environment Report that it aims to "use the minimum weight of packaging necessary for the packaging functions to be met". But its Maple & Pecan Crisp packets were only 40 per cent full. Mike Childs, Senior Waste Campaigner at Friends of the Earth claims that: "Despite all their green rhetoric, supermarkets are scamming consumers and creating excessive waste through over-packaging products."

disease. France, Spain and Portugal have the lowest rates. Food continues to be produced and marketed in this way because consumers are ignorant about the way their food is produced. It is not helped by labelling: terms such as "fresh", or "farmhouse" are meaningless and have no legal status. Indeed recent research by the Food Commission has shown that some products described as "fresh" on the label actually have a shelf life of up to two years. But without consumer pressure, there is little incentive for the manufacturers and retailers to change their way of doing business. It is, after all, highly profitable.

Super stores? >

Supermarkets have had a devastating impact on local food stores like grocers, butchers, bakers and fishmongers. As many as 200,000 of the UK's independent food stores – half the total – may have closed down in the past ten years alone. This reduces local employment and the local skill base as well as removing villages' informal meeting places for a chat and gossip. Recently the National Federation of Women's Institutes has attacked supermarkets for destroying village life. "They are taking trade away from local shops, which are the backbone of these communities. Local shops cannot compete with supermarkets, but it is a vicious cycle, it is the local shops which offer convenience shopping for people with children, pensioners and those who can't drive, or don't have access to a car," says spokeswoman Sangeeta Haindl.

When a new supermarket opens in a rural area it will close all village shops within a seven-mile radius, claims Alan Wyle of the Sussex Rural Community Council, in the Liberal Democrats' report "Checking Out The Supermarkets" which took a hard look at competition amongst the retailing giants. One example in this report cites the farm shop at Aldercarr Farm, in Suffolk, which saw takings fall by half in the week that a Tesco opened outside Stowmarket, five miles away. Not long after two local greengrocers closed.

Can't shop local >>

Peter Brock, Research Fellow at Exeter University's Centre for Energy and the Environment, is well aware of the problems choosing to shop at superstores causes. "Having a car is a fantastic liberator. But even when people are aware of the problem it's difficult not to be party to it. I just wish there was a simple answer. Where I live there isn't a shop around - what were there have closed because people use their cars to drive to the supermarket - so it's a Catch-22 situation."

As Peter Brock's dilemma shows (see box: Can't shop local), we have lost much of the choice we once had. Although the supermarkets stock thousands of different "lines" - many small producers of regional speciality foods have been driven out of business, and many traditional varieties of fruits and vegetables are no longer available because they cannot be produced in sufficient quantity to fulfil the supermarkets' stringent cosmetic and quantity requirements. Meanwhile, not everyone is enjoying the range of food, or healthy food at all. The much talked-about changes in the British diet vary widely across British society: for those families subsisting on state benefits, the average of £2.37 allowed per adult, per day, for food (1996 figures) does not buy a lot of fresh vegetables, much less a lunchtime snack of ciabatta and roasted peppers.

Shelf life >

Inside the supermarket too, the choice is not as great as it first might seem. An average Sainsbury's, for instance, stocks around 20,000 different product lines. But having a dozen different kinds of margarine to choose from doesn't make any of them much more appetising. As Ian Egginton-Metters, Director of the Federation of

City Farms and Community Gardens points out: "There is no choice in supermarkets, or most greengrocers. Usually what's on offer is just one variety of carrot. If you always buy that type of carrot, then you will never know what other carrots taste or even look like."

Supermarkets also demand such standardised specifications for their fruit and vegetables – usually according to cosmetic factors like size, shape and appearance – that the number of varieties on offer has sharply declined. Vegetables, like lettuces, are more likely to be selected for sale because they match a specified colour swatch than because they taste good.

The tragedy is that there are hundreds of different tasty British varieties. Take apples, many of which, with wide variations in size, shape, colour and flavour, used to be available in different stores in different parts of the country at different times of year. Nowadays, supermarkets stock perhaps three or four kinds all year round – and fairly tasteless they all are too. The supermarkets' demand for unblemished looks and standard sizes also leads to huge wastage – around 20 per cent of all produce is discarded after passing its sell by date. Supermarkets have faced considerably more criticism since the 1996 BSE scare. Despite plummeting prices for animals at auction, supermarket prices have remained unchanged. It makes you wonder why supermarkets insist that they are good value.

Because the big supermarkets make most of their sourcing decisions nationally, they cannot deal with small, specialist producers making local varieties of cheese, meat and baked goods. Local producers of many of Britain's delicious traditional cheeses, for example, get by-passed. The problem is that they cannot produce enough to tight deadlines, and are not prepared to meet supermarket specifications dictated by issues of space rather than quality.

As a result, many local products have become harder and harder to buy – even in the region where they are produced – and some die out altogether. This does not bother the supermarkets, as they prefer to deal with the smallest number of suppliers possible. Indeed at the 1997 European Fresh Produce convention delegates heard predictions that each supermarket chain hoped to limit the number of distributors to: "No more than three per commodity". In other words, three suppliers of apples, three suppliers of tomatoes, three suppliers of cauliflowers, and so on.

Supermarkets contribute to other serious environmental problems too. One consequence of centralised supermarket buying and distribution systems is that food is trucked hundreds of miles around the country to and from centralised distribution depots. Roughly the same total amount of food is now transported at least 50 per cent further around the UK than it was 20 years ago. This phenomenon is often referred to as "food miles". The additional transport creates extra air pollution and road congestion.

Food miles are carried to greater extremes by the supermarkets' desire to offer a complete range of fruit and vegetables year-round. Strawberries are flown from the USA, asparagus from Peru, green beans from Kenya – all demanding enormous quantities of aviation fuel. Air transport is now the fastest growing source of carbon

Go to the top >>

"Supermarkets do see all the benefits of local food, both for the environment and from their own perspective. They're not questioning whether stocking locally-grown food is a good thing or not," says Nicola Davis from the BioRegional Food Group who recently completed a feasibility study on local food networks. "They know it could save them money and they see that every time they do local promotions, sales go up. But nothing happens. It's possibly just a matter of going to the highest level, to the director, and getting them to spread the message through the company and to the buyers."

dioxide emissions – the principal cause of the dangerous climate change that we now see causing floods, droughts and storms worldwide. And the further food is transported, the more protective packaging it requires, creating more waste for already over-filled landfill sites.

Meanwhile there are transport consequences closer to home as well. Most new supermarkets are built on the edge of town, with poor or non-existent public transport access. One survey found that 97 per cent of all supermarket shoppers use a car to get there – thus burning more fuel, causing more air pollution and congesting our streets. And building new roads and supermarkets eats up yet more of our disappearing countryside.

Summing up >

As people begin to realise how the big stores' buying polices can have harmful effects on farming and local economies the supermarket chains have started to face criticism. The key areas of concern are the loss of specialist food stores in local communities; the disappearance of regional specialities because of the supermarkets commitment to centralised buying; the growth in food miles and the lack of help to developing world farmers.

The success of FOE's campaign to stop supermarkets using GM ingredients proves that individuals can change both company and local government policy. There have been other successes too: GM food has been banned from many school canteens; the UK's top 23 restaurants have demanded a freeze on GM food and crops and the Government has been stopped from using an illegal scheme to fast-track approval of GM seeds for growing in the UK. All this shows that if we want real food we can tell the supermarkets to stock it - if enough people make a fuss, they will.

What you can do >>
Use our supermarket quiz, on page 90, to see if your store is making any effort to stock real food.

⑪ Section B

Check out real food

Chapter 5

Out in the fields

When Janet Walker left her job as a social worker her husband, Tom, gave her two large white weaner pigs to raise. That was three years ago and since then the family has been eating its own home-grown meat. "People say, 'How can you eat something that you have raised?'' But I say, 'How can you eat anything that you know has been grown in really awful conditions?','" says Walker. "It's important that children know that animals get killed and then we eat them. When my 10-year-old son went to the abattoir with our pig he saw a dead cow for the first time, and was shocked by how huge it was, and how it smelt. Now when he eats beef he knows where it comes from."

The Walker family decided to make their own bacon, pork and sausages after a couple of years successfully growing most of their own organic vegetables. "We were worried about the environment and though most of our extended family are vegetarian, we are not. We were not happy about the way animals were reared so we felt if we were not raising our own food then we could not eat it," explains Walker who keeps pigs, hens, geese on the four-acre plot in Essex.

Few people have the energy, land, skills or time to grow all their own food, even if many would like to do so. But that doesn't mean shoppers are content with the food which is currently on offer, especially as they begin to realise that the cornucopia of products on offer are not as healthy as they may at first seem. What people want is to be able to choose fresh food that does us, our families and the environment no long-term harm.

The good news is that some farmers are trying to farm in a more sensitive way. And those are the farmers whom shoppers could be supporting.

Although Richard Howard-Vyse still relies on chemicals, he is careful to make sure wildlife have food and habitat on the 1,100 acres he farms in Malton, North Yorkshire. "I regard conservation as part of life, but farming is a business and we have to sell a product. If our potatoes or wheat are blighted then we can't do that." What he can do is tempt wildlife on to the farm. "I love to encourage the grey partridge and plovers on to my farm," says Howard-Vyse. "But now there are no spring crops you don't see the great flocks of plovers feeding in the early morning that you would see 30 years ago. As we have to have set-aside I thought let's be imaginative with it, lets give the wildlife we've got better habitat."

To do this he turned his set-aside corridors into a tempting habitat for birds, providing short-growing rye grass for birds to sun themselves and tall-growing seed crops for food as well as cover from danger. He is also taking advantage of Countryside Stewardship Scheme grants to increase the amount of hedgerow on his land. And his dedication has paid off: not just by attracting wildlife but also securing his family farm the prestigious Broadoak Farming Silver Lapwing Award, run by the Farming & Wildlife Advisory Group, in 1998.

Realistically, even with massive demand for organic food and better government support, it would take many years for even a quarter of British farmland to convert to organic production. However, there are simpler targets that we could aim for in the meantime. There is a wide range of more environmentally responsible farming methods which while not fully organic, could bring many of the benefits of organic food in terms of consumer confidence in food safety, lessened impact on the environment, and revitalised rural economies.

One example is the UK's system of Environmentally Sensitive Areas (ESAs), areas designated by the Government as eligible for special grants to encourage traditional, environmentally-friendly farming methods. Studies in ESAs such as the South Downs and the Pennine Dales have shown significant local job gains. Nearly 10 per cent of UK farmland is eligible for ESA funds. New jobs benefit rural economies, as does the spending of the organic farmers themselves, thus helping to safeguard local shops and services. And consumers get delicious, traditionally-reared beef and lamb. The Ministry of Agriculture's voluntary Countryside Stewardship Scheme has seen similar benefits in jobs for conservation-friendly farming practices. Unfortunately, the schemes are all entirely voluntary and payments small.

But it is in Sweden that environmentally-friendly but non-organic agriculture has been carried furthest. As early as 1986, the Swedish government recognised the growing threat posed by chemical agriculture. It introduced a range of measures to support what is know as *Kretslopp* (loosely, "farming with nature") – including a reduction in antibiotic use for poultry and livestock by over half. The use of "Integrated Crop Management" systems that rely on natural predators, better targeting of smaller quantities of pesticides and different planting patterns has greatly reduced the use of pesticides. Now, Swedish consumer confidence in food is high and agriculture is financially stronger than Britain's ailing, chemical-driven farming sector.

Elsewhere in Europe there are other methods at work that British farmers could benefit from in changing the way they produce food and marketing it to the public. Producer co-operatives, for example, can help farmers market new products and process their products more locally – a problem at present for organic goods such as eggs. Co-operatives are still rare in the UK but widespread in France and other countries. It is a method which has been turned into an art form by the Japanese which run more than 600 co-ops used by 16 million people.

In some ways the food co-op is a variation on the vegetable box buying schemes (described in Chapter 6). Co-ops are membership organisations that buy in bulk to lower the costs of food. They can source their food more locally than supermarkets, and exert consumer power more directly over food suppliers. In Japan groups of families put in bulk orders for environmentally-friendly food, which is then delivered regularly. Some are now large enterprises:

the Seikatsu Club, for example, has over 200,000 members and an annual spending budget of £160 million.

Co-op buying can also benefit farmers. For example Kentish Garden, a nationwide fruit marketing co-op, has just introduced an innovative new computer system to enable supermarkets to see the availability of produce linked to the nearest regional distribution centre, which reduces the distance food has to travel. Unbelievably the old system simply showed what was available so produce was allocated at random. Although this has been done to save costs it has clear environmental benefits.

Another variation of the co-op is "subscription farming", where a group of consumers put up a subscription at the start of the year to take a share in the harvest. To date these have only been tried in the UK and US.

Grow your own >

There is also considerable potential for people to grow more of their own food – not just in their gardens, but in allotments, city farms and community gardens. Locally grown food is better for the environment because it uses less transport and creates less waste such as packaging. Community-grown food also has multiple social benefits, allowing local people to get involved in growing their own food, and providing a means of social inclusion for marginalised groups such as the unemployed and ethnic minorities. There are now dozens of such schemes operating in the UK including 68 city farms and more than 500 community gardens. And there are still thousands of council-owned allotments.

One organisation helping urban growers is the Federation of City Farms and Community Gardens (FCFCG). "Unless people know about gardening they need support. If you suggest people grow their own food to groups which have not got any experience you are either regarded as mad or with a lot of time on your hands. But many people do grow flowers and it is possible to also grow edible plants. You can get some aesthetic beauty and grow something

Asian tastes >>

In Bradford, for instance, the Bangladesh Porishad Horticulture Projects have enabled retired and unemployed Bangladeshi men and women to grow vegetables on allotments. As well as helping provide fresh Asian vegetables for their families, the projects have had social benefits: they have helped give people confidence and status, as well as exercise, and saving them money.

good to eat by thinking about what you grow and where you grow it," says Ian Egginton-Metters, Director of FCFCG, who runs workshops to show people how to plant edibles in the most restricted spaces, including window boxes and hanging baskets.

Urban growing has huge environmental benefits. As Charles Secrett, Director of Friends of the Earth, points out: "Buying locally produced, healthy food is one of the best things every household can do to benefit their health and help the environment. Locally sourced food reduces air pollution, traffic generating 'food miles', sustains local jobs and is grown as it should be, in season."

One company which has managed to help local employment and attract shoppers is yoghurt specialist Rachel's Dairy in Aberystwyth. "The market is growing at such a rate that we are unable to keep up with demand," explains Rachel Rowlands who, with her husband Gareth, set up Rachel's Dairy. "We need to encourage farmers in our area to produce organic milk as we have to import milk from the continent to satisfy the demand. I feel there is something inherently wrong in transporting milk across the continent to Wales, which in the long-term is not desirable in either environmental or economic terms."

Rachel is still puzzled about why there were no grants available and no banks would help her set up the company back in the mid

1980s. Now more than 10 years on the dairy is processing around 70,000 litres per week and employs 58 people. The company was recently acquired by the US Horizon Organic Dairy, which plans to expand immediately to meet the consumer demand for organics. "There is an unstoppable growth in demand for naturally produced food and people are increasingly concerned about production methods," says Rachel. "Today the benefits of organics are much more widely discussed in the media. shoppers now have far greater choice and many opt for organic because it is food that they feel they can trust, and they feel good about buying it for their families."

Summing up >

Because there is likely to be a shortfall in the supply of UK-produced organic food for some time, and because of the supermarkets' distribution systems, organic food alone is not enough to create a sustainable food production system. For that, we need a far more localised system of production, distribution and sale. This need not exclude supermarkets: local supermarket branches could be given far more power to source food locally, as they already do for instance in Denmark. Nor need it be exclusively organic. Organic production is starting from a very low base, especially in the UK, and we will be mostly dependent on non-organic foods for some time.

A more localised system will need to build on many new – or perhaps old – distribution and retail systems in order to cut down on energy use. That's where schemes like vegetable box delivery schemes and farmers markets, described in the next two chapters, work so well. This is your chance to show the politicians that they have misjudged the public's taste buds, help the environment, and provide your family with tasty, real food.

What you can do >>

To help you get your hands on real food, support FOE's Real Food Charter on page 94.

Chapter 6

Go organic: a consumer revolution >>

Wednesday is peak time for mid-week working blues. Pressure is mounting in the office, so there's no time to shop and nothing worth eating when you do eventually make it home. At least that's how it used to be for Richard Allen in Friends of the Earth's computer department until he joined a vegetable delivery service which drops off fresh boxes of seasonal fruit and vegetables every Wednesday afternoon at the office.

"I was thinking I ought to get organised and eat more organic stuff," says Allen, "because it can be quite difficult to get hold of at my local shops. I'd thought about signing up to a vegetable box scheme doing home deliveries, but because of my work schedule it was never going to be convenient. The vegetables from Scragoak Farm are really good and I find the selection makes me experiment more when I cook. There can be treats as well, recently I found a pot of purple basil in my box. It's been delicious, even more mundane vegetables, like the carrots and potatoes, seem really wholesome."

The inspiration behind the Scragoak Farm vegetable delivery service which supplies Friends of the Earth's London office is Steve Christopher. Christopher, who works with Pitfield Brewery, used to drive past Scragoak's organic farm shop on his weekly trip to visit an organic vineyard supplier in Sussex. He offered to bring back greens for his friends in London and soon found that he had a growing shopping list. This inspired him to put the arrangement on a more formal footing, by negotiating a bulk discount with the farm. He now delivers fat boxes of organic vegetables packed in Sussex to around 100 London customers each week - including office groups.

Vegetable delivery services are helping people change the way we buy food - and introducing many households to seasonal, organic produce. It is a simple idea, and one used by all sorts of people –

from well-known food writers, to families wanting a regular supply of fresh organic vegetables for their young children without the hassle of having to track it down in a small corner of the supermarket.

Vegetable boxes do not just make shopping easier - they also help farms guarantee a local market. The idea is that a farm or group of suppliers puts together a selection of locally-produced fresh fruit and vegetables each week and delivers a full box (or bag) to members of the scheme, or to a convenient central collection point, such as a friendly health food shop, community centre or one of the members' own homes. Back in 1991 FOE members in Exeter helped start a vegetable box scheme supplied by nearby Northwood Farm. "Throughout Exeter there were six or seven drop-off points so that everyone who subscribed went to someone's house to pick up their veggies. It was incredibly good value getting so much good food," says computer consultant Maurice Spurway. "I liked getting local fresh food and knowing that by buying it I was supporting the people who produced it. If you buy in Sainsbury's you often have no idea where it came from – it could have travelled miles."

Five years on around 400 organic vegetable delivery services can be found throughout the country, organised by a variety of volunteer groups, farms, co-operatives, companies and stores, delivering to an estimated 50,000 families each week. These groups normally offer different size boxes, and their produce is usually organic, which is why a third of the UK's organic growers are involved in box schemes. It is also, of course, seasonal. You don't get any strawberries in January, although you do get more types of root vegetable than you probably realised existed, including British classics like swede and turnip. Prices are generally lower than organic produce in shops, since there is no middleman, and can be lower than conventionally-produced. And because you develop a relationship with the producer of your food, this is food you know you can trust.

Wash and go >>

After Julie Brown left her job at FOE's London office she decided to set up a vegetable box scheme. Five years on Growing Communities, a company limited by guarantee, is now supplying more than 100 households in Hackney with a weekly bag of fresh vegetables and free range eggs. Most weeks the bags are stuffed full, but inclement weather and hungry pests can cause hiccups. "If your vegetable box scheme has a direct link with a particular farm you may find that the quality of goods vary because crops fail, or the weather is unpredictable," says Julie. "Some people find getting a box of seasonal vegetables difficult. It depends whether you are the sort of person who is inspired by broad beans every week for several months, and then don't see them again for another nine months, or finds it compromises your cooking. You have to learn to cook what you have in the bag, rather than putting the same vegetables in the pot day in and day out. The benefits are not just the taste, but that it opens your eyes to the different seasons."

As the demand for real food grows, vegetable delivery schemes have become so popular that many even operate a waiting list. It is worth looking around anyway as the schemes are extraordinarily varied, ranging from the Birmingham-based Organic Roundabout to the cycle deliveries of Green Adventure in South London. Some only operate in glut seasons (the summer), some expect you to do the collecting and some have strict rulings about food miles.

As food writer Nigel Slater points out, ordering a vegetable box has many advantages: "What means most to me is not the convenience (I could, at a push, survive without setting foot in the greengrocers or a supermarket) but the fact that the delivery keeps me in touch with the seasons - I can see how the basics differ or disappear throughout the year." It's a point another well-known food writer, Lynda Brown, also highlights: "Such schemes are also the most environmentally friendly and sustainable way to buy vegetables, while forging that valuable link with the land that modern lifestyles have lost."

Why buy organic? >

The staggering growth of interest in organic food is nothing less than a consumer revolution. But it is a revolution that has been born out of distrust for the modern methods of farming which brought us salmonella in eggs, the BSE cattle crisis and other food scares. In the UK, organic food retail sales were an estimated £40 million in 1996/97, around the time of the first outbreaks of BSE. By 1997 the market had grown to £267 million and it could be worth £500 million by 2000. Demand for certain products has been staggering. For example, over the past two years organic dairy sales have increased by 250 per cent and organic meat sales by 189 per cent.

But it is baby food which has seen the biggest growth (400 per cent), perhaps because there is so much research showing that babies, toddlers and children are more vulnerable to pesticide residues in food and drink than adults - and that because of children's immature body systems; smaller size; higher food needs and restricted choices they are more heavily exposed to them. Indeed influential foodie author Joanna Blythman reveals in her book *The Food Our Children Eat* that one child in 20 consumes unsafe levels of organophosphate chemicals every day.

Although babies can be fed home-made organic food there are now several organic pre-prepared brands as well as more and more organic products turning up on supermarket shelves. By summer 1999, Sainsbury's alone was selling nearly £2 million of organic products a week and was offering more than 400 product lines - a tenfold increase since 1997.

Baby love >>

Lizzie Vann and Jane Dick set up Baby Organix - the first range of organic baby food in the UK - in 1992. Their aim was to provide food which was free of additives, preservatives, added sugar, processing aids and fillers. The company's guiding principle is that all food should be simple, tasty and nutritious. All ingredients are organic and GM free. The concept of tasty, healthy, organic-filled jars has been a staggering success. At the end of 1998 the organic baby food market was worth more than £16.5 million and Baby Organix held half of that market. The company's taste trials - happy babies in high chairs tucking into baby mush - are regularly seen on news bulletins.

The aim of organic farming is to farm using natural methods and products in order to produce healthy crops and animals in a way which does the minimum damage to the environment.

Organic is a legal category, enforced in the UK by seven independent organisations which are licensed to certify food as organic. One of the best known certifiers is the Bristol-based Soil Association. All are regulated by the Government's UK Register of Organic Food Standards (UKROFS). Organic food must be:

>> Produced without artificial pesticides or fertilisers. Instead, organic farmers use natural fertilisers such as manure, and natural methods of pest control such as natural insect predators, and careful weeding and mulching.

>> Produced with care for the environment and the soil. For instance, farmers must rotate crops rather than keep fields under constant cultivation, and must practise soil conservation.

>> Produced in conditions which are humane and as natural as possible for animals. Animals must not be fed industrially produced feed supplements, or artificial drugs except if they are seriously sick. Animals have access to the outdoors and are allowed to express natural behaviour patterns – in hens, for example, scratching the ground, preening, nesting and perching, none of which are possible in battery farms. They are fed on natural feedstuffs.

>> Free of any genetically modified materials. To become organic, a farm has to undergo the process of conversion, which takes two to three years depending on the crop. Products from farms undergoing conversion are increasingly available; they do not yet meet organic standards, but are worth buying if there is no organic alternative, as they offer some of the benefits of organic and their

---

Doing it my way >>

As Chair of the Soil Association Helen Browning has a lot to live up too. Not only is she involved in the charity's policy decisions; she also farms 1,300 acres of land organically at Eastbrook Farm, Wiltshire. Eastbrook Farm's enterprises include two dairy herds, veal calves, beef cattle, pigs and sheep; and cereals, feed crops and vegetables. All farm livestock, and also that purchased from other organic farms in growing numbers, is sold through multiple retailers, a nationwide home delivery service, and through the farm shop. Since converting to organic production in 1986, Browning has proved that organic farming is both profitable and viable on a large scale. She has maintained the highest standards required of organic produce. The farm's veal calves live as natural lives as possible, in the fields with their mothers, as do her pigs, raised outdoors in spacious enclosures.

---

producers are going through a difficult stage in changing their production methods. After being verified by a certification body, organic farms and produce are inspected yearly to check that the strict standards are being maintained.

The major principle underlying organic food manufacture is that organic production should be separated from non-organic production by time or clearly defined space. This is to prevent non-organic ingredients contaminating an organic product.

Money matters >

Although the organic business is booming, many farmers claim that they can't afford to convert - and with good reason. In April 1999 the annual sum available to aid farmers make organic conversion was quadrupled, yet it is still the paltry figure of £6.2 million when compared with the amount MAFF spends on research and development for industrial farming (£125 million) or the Government's 1998 spend on agricultural biotechnology (£52 million).

This means that though some farms and firms producing organic food become very well known – such as the dairy products produced by Yeo Valley - many food manufacturers have problems getting hold of 100 per cent organic ingredients.

"We've got nothing to hide with our ingredients," says Graham Orton, Marketing Manager of the family brewers Samuel Smith in Tadcaster, North Yorkshire. Indeed the label lists even the seaweed findings making the UK's second certified organic beer, Sam Smith's Organic Best Ale, one of the few suitable for strict vegans. But producing such a beer in Britain is not easy. There is only one commercial producer of organic hops, in Kent, and just one grower of organic malted barley, in southern Scotland. As a result the company has to import organic hops for its Organic Best Ale.

The irony is that organic farming can bring substantial benefits to the rural economy as well as to consumers. It is estimated that on average its labour demands are 10 per cent higher than conventional farming, and in some sectors, such as strawberry growers, it can be much higher still. A number of studies have shown that organic production of beef, poultry and eggs, as well as vegetables and orchard fruits substantially increases the number of farm jobs.

For example at Helen Browning's Eastbrook Farm, organic conversion has seen staff jobs grow from eight full-time staff to 14 full-time farm staff and a further 10 at Eastbrook Farm Organic Meats, its direct sales shop and mail order business. On average farmers estimated that the impact of conversion to organic farming saw a 23 per cent increase in employment. In Wales research also showed that organic production can offer greater on-farm employment in marketing and processing as well as better labour incomes from farming.

Some people are put off organic food because they feel it is expensive. Organic products can cost anywhere from 10 to 60 per cent more than the conventional version – or even more if you compare organic meat and the cheapest, lowest-quality economy versions in supermarkets. A 1998 Soil Association/MORI poll found that nearly half of shoppers associated the word "organic" with "expensive".

They are right: organic food costs more to produce. This is because it is generally produced on a smaller scale, and is more labour-intensive. Farmers who give their animals a good life rather than cramming them into dank sheds and feeding them antibiotics cannot compete with large-sale factory farming operations. Because they care for the environment, organic farmers do not "externalise" environmental costs such as the water pollution or health problems caused by conventional farming. Indeed if conventional producers were forced to pay the full costs of their chemical use on farms, instead of dumping them on to taxpayers, the price difference with organic food would be far smaller.

However, as organic farming becomes more mainstream, prices are expected to drop.

Consumers have enormous power in changing the food system. Supermarkets do respond to consumer pressure – as they have, for example, by starting to offer a wider range of organic goods. But for there to be real change through the whole food system, we need political change at a higher level too.

One of the main reasons that organic farming still has such a small share of UK agriculture, despite its benefits, is that organic farmers gets minimal support from government. Payments to farmers to encourage them to convert to organic production, a potentially risky move that takes up to three years, have been among the lowest in Europe, although they have been recently raised to a level that is roughly the EU average. Britain is also one of only three EU countries whose governments do not pay continuing maintenance subsidies to organic farmers in recognition of the long-term benefits of organic farming to the environment and rural society.

Government support for farming has until now concentrated almost entirely on helping large-scale, intensive agriculture. While organic farmers have received little help, the UK Government and the EU have provided subsidies and grants for a range of destructive practices from heavy pesticide use to tearing up ancient hedgerows. This is perverse, because 50 years of subsidies to conventional farmers have produced little except rural unemployment and a few rich arable farmers. They have not averted the latest slide in agricultural commodity prices. Indeed the BSE crisis, the greatest post-war crisis in UK agriculture, was caused by government policy: the then Conservative Government relaxed regulations on animal feed production to please a few major manufacturers, allowing dangerous proteins into the food chain.

The UK Government needs to develop a strategy for developing our organic sector, with clear targets and policies to achieve them. Friends of the Earth has proposed a target of 30 per cent of land to be under organic management by 2010. The UK's organic farmers deserve maintenance payments, both to compete with other EU producers and to help the environment. There is a trade-off: more money in subsidies would be balanced by lower costs for environmental clean-up.

Government could also give organic farmers, and especially those farmers interested in organic conversion, more practical support in the form of advice and professional expertise. The Government set up the Organic Conversion Information Service in 1996, run by the Soil Association and the Organic Advisory Service at the leading organic research farm, Elm Farm Research Centre, but it has been heavily oversubscribed, with 4,500 enquiries in its first two years of operation and a waiting list.

Government also needs to increase its funding of research into organic and sustainable farming. Money could be raised by a tax on pesticides and fertilisers, and by diverting public money currently used to support unsustainable farming methods. Government scientists currently working on conventional agricultural research and in biotechnology could be redeployed into sustainable farming research.

Summing up >

It is so hard to find fresh locally-grown vegetables in the supermarkets; such a drag reading mystifying descriptions of ingredients printed in tiny writing on the label and so irritating coping with excess package wrapped around so much of the food we buy that many people are already trying out the new ways of shopping outlined above. It's not just vegetable box delivery services which are growing rapidly, there are farm shops, farmers markets, food co-ops and e-commerce. Statistics show that in 1997 more than 70 per cent of all consumer spending on fruit was in supermarkets, as was more than two-thirds of all spending on bread and eggs. It doesn't have to be this way now there is so much choice about the places that shoppers can find real food.

Government is also supporting the biggest threat to organic farming, the frighteningly fast growth of GM crops at test sites. These are supposed to be managed so that the environment is kept safe, but how can strips a few metres wide be considered to be enough protection from pollinating insects? It is not just consumer groups and neighbouring farmers which are worried, the UK's beekeepers are particularly concerned about the effect this could have on their hives.

"A lot of beekeepers are very sensitive about the health cache that honey has," explains Adrian Waring, General Secretary of the British Beekeepers Association. "People think of honey as a pure, natural food and beekeepers want to keep it that way. But how can we with GM crops? We're just not being told enough. Now that GM plants are resistant to herbicides, companies, like Monsanto, are going to have to take notice of bees. Bees fly as far as they have to. That could be two miles out and two miles back, but it can also be much further. Bees aren't going to be stopped by a little strip."

It seems astonishing that the growth of a sustainable industry like organic farming could be put into such jeopardy by a government which has cosied up to the biotechnology industry.

What you can do >>

Find out more about how to identify organic food by using our Good Label Guide on page 89.

Chapter 7

Retail therapy:
changing the way we buy food >>

In Islington, the heart of Tony Blair country, farmers are gathering. This isn't an historical re-enactment of Islington's long-forgotten agrarian past or a meeting of disgruntled flat cap wearers outraged by the Government's lack of understanding of country matters. No, this is Islington's regular Sunday farmers' market and it's attracting plenty of punters. Some seem bemused by the stalls of fresh strawberries, organic beetroot and English wines which are grown less than 100 miles from Islington, but many more are relishing being able to buy genuinely fresh produce from the very farmers who spend the rest of the week tending crops and stock on their farms. If a farmers' market can compete with antiques buying and the Tesco Metro in such a trendy corner of London, surely this is a sign that many shoppers are delighting in finding new ways of buying their food?

Despite the astonishing growth of the organic market, organic farming still represents a small fraction of the UK's food production. At the beginning of 1998 there was just over 100,000 hectares of organically managed farmland in the UK, just 0.8 per cent of the total. This compares with an EU average of 1.33 per cent, and close to 10 per cent of land in some countries such as Austria. Just two per cent of total fresh produce sold in the UK is organic.

As a result supermarkets have to import a large proportion of their organic food from overseas – 70 per cent of the total organic food on sale in the UK is imported. Sainsbury's, for example, imports 75 per cent of its organic produce. Although it can source carrots from Britain, the giant retailer has to buy organic carrots from Holland, Denmark and Israel. Organic apples are currently more likely to come from the USA, Argentina or New Zealand – despite the fact that England is naturally an apple-growing country.

Because of the way supermarkets distribute their stock even British grown organic food can be transported around the country excessively. For example in Evesham, Worcestershire, two supermarkets sell organic produce, some of which is grown on farms just 1.5km away. However to get the vegetables from the farm to the supermarket's shelves, the produce must first travel to a co-operative in Herefordshire; then to a packing station in Dyfed, Wales; then to a distribution depot south of Manchester; and finally back to the Evesham stores.

To try and beat this jet-set mindset, many shoppers are trying out new ways of shopping like farmers' markets, farm shops, e-commerce and home delivery. The goods may not always be organic, but they will be sold by the people who know all about real food because they grew the crop. The number of food miles travelled from farm to plate will be few, and that will ensure the freshest possible quality - factors which are all good for our health, taste buds and the environment.

Farmers' markets >

Farmers' markets, which are just like street markets except it is farmers selling the goods direct to consumers, have been popular shopping hot spots for years in the US, where there are now 2,400. However the UK has been slow to copy their blueprint - the first British farmers' market was set up in Bath in 1997. But in 1998 many pilot farmers' markets were trialed all over the UK and were so successful that they have become regular fixtures attracting a large number of loyal shoppers.

The advantage for the farmer is that they generate higher profits and improved cash flows. For the shopper food is fresher. Early risers do get the best deals. For example, at a recent Winchester market around 10,000 people turned up and cleared out half the stalls by 11am. One stall holder at the new Islington farmers' market, in London, reckons the experience makes it worth getting out of bed early on a Sunday. "It's wonderful. There are the smells of fresh bread, perfect strawberries and raspberries. It's a chance to buy fresh, delicious food all in one place and from people who know all about it," says John Chapple who co-ordinates the West Middlesex Beekeepers stall piled high with honey produced by London bees.

Holmfirth Farmers' Market was inspired by a Local Agenda 21 initiative and has been so successful that it's even won a UK Food Group award. Originally held at Huddersfield, making it the first farmers market in the north of England, there are now around 30 regular stall holders offering goods as diverse as locally made meat pies to locally bottled Pennine spring water on Sundays from April to December. "The market gives local producers a direct line to local consumers. It reduces food miles, helps local businesses (only those operating within 40 miles radius of the market are eligible) and gives shoppers the chance to buy fresher food," says organiser Gerald Riley.

These days there are nearly 100 farmers' markets being held regularly round the country and many more are due to be set up. The only snag is that they require skilled organisers with enough time to kick-start the process. "I've been involved in lots of things but the most complicated to arrange was the farmers market," admits Tim Crabtree, an economist, who co-ordinates the West Dorset Food and Land Trust which organises two markets a month at Bridport and Dorchester in Devon. "We had to find stall holders to come, a venue and attract shoppers," he explains. But the pilot market at Bridport, held at the Arts Centre right in the middle of the town, was so successful that a year on more than 1,000 people visit the stalls. "At first we had just 15 stall holders, but now we have a list of 44 traders," adds Crabtree.

Crabtree is trying to develop a range of initiatives to encourage people to eat more healthily and shop closer to home. His organisation has already secured funding to make a food garden at St Andrew's Preschool, in Bridport, and has plans to lease land as managed work spaces, complete with polytunnels to give agricultural college graduates a chance to build a business and sell their produce at the farmers' market.

The organisation is not the only one encouraging local producers to turn up with the highest quality goods. "Supermarkets do not offer the best deal for producers," says Sean Levy of the National Farmers Union. "There's enormous potential for farmers with marketing initiative to develop other ways of selling, especially direct to the public. They should recognise people's consumer nature and make the purchase interesting to them," he suggests. "People like buying food in a different way but the quality has to be good. Producers will not get away with selling a second rate product."

"If people know how to produce food they will be more interested in buying food locally rather than being satisfied with microwaved crap from the supermarket," adds Crabtree. "Unless you have tasted a fresh picked pea or a raspberry picked straight from the bush, why would you be interested in buying at a farmers' market?"

Farm shops >

Of course, you can buy direct from farms, and increasing numbers of farmers are setting up farm shops to meet this demand. Like the vegetable box delivery schemes and the farmers' markets, the stock in farm shops varies hugely. Some have just a few lines available and others are packed with a vast range of goods and worthy of a day trip. In general if you pass a farm shop it is worth looking in - and if there's one near you, think yourself lucky. Not only can you expect to find, at the very least, some locally produced goods - from vegetables to cakes - you can also expect to find the prices very competitive. Many lines will be 15-20 per cent cheaper than at the greengrocers.

Snail mail and e-commerce >

Trying to track down certain products such as organic meat can be hard, but access to the internet can make the search considerably quicker. Internet shopping, sometimes known as e-commerce, is still in its infancy, but even if you are reluctant to part with credit card details on the net, access to the world wide web can help provide instant information about product availability and price from a particular farm. This is an area where the smallest suppliers to the largest supermarkets are exploring.

One fan is Tony Yates, who claims internet shopping has distinct advantages for the time-pressed. "Some six or so years ago my partner and I decided that we would stop having a car and only use cabs when there was no practical alternative," says Yates, who works at Brunel University, London. "One major example of this was bulk food/grocery supermarket shopping trips. We find that home delivery services offer a more environmentally friendly option as one van trip delivers several households worth of car trips. It also means that we never have to get stuck in jams on our way to the supermarket, trudge around it with 1,000 other irritated trolley ragers, queue at the checkout and struggle to get home again."

Doorstep delivery >

Home deliveries are not a new invention. It is only during the past couple of decades that door-to-door deliveries - the wet fish seller, baker and grocer - came to a stop. But recently some goods, like wines, beer, organic meat and exotic specialities, such as chilli peppers are now available through mail order. You can also buy a large range of fair-traded goods from Traidcraft's catalogue.

And there's still that old-fashioned method of organising your life so that milk is delivered to the door. "Getting milk on the doorstep is so convenient," points out Hubert Elsworth who has run a milk round for the past 30 years from Penistone, Yorkshire. "We can't compete with the supermarket price but our milk is fresh and locally produced." And you don't have to drive a car to pick up a drop of milk for your breakfast muesli.

Summing up >

By using local shops, and sampling the goods produced by local farmers, in season, you are getting your hands on food that has come the shortest possible distance from farmers' gate to dinner plate. This means your meal has caused less pollution because the food miles are minimal. It means a reduction in waste for landfill sites, because the items you have chosen will not need to be deeply wrapped in protective layers to prevent them from being bruised, squashed or spilt on the journey. It also means you are helping to support local livelihoods by giving more of the profit directly to the farmer. Best of all it means you are choosing real food which is as fresh as possible.

What you can do >>

See the Contacts section, page 95, for groups which are helping ensure we can get real food.

Chapter 8

Staying in store >>

Doctors and nutritionists want us to eat better. They advise that everyone should eat five portions of fruit and vegetable a day as part of a healthy diet. But as more people become aware of how intensively farmed our daily diet has become, many decide that it's not good enough throwing over-packaged veggies into a supermarket trolley. What they want is tasty food, grown with as little chemical input as possible - at least that is how Cathy Chapman, her partner Mark and their daughters Mae and Caitlin felt.

Cathy used to grow much of their own fruit and vegetables at home in a village near York. But she couldn't grow it all. At first she topped up the family's food needs by driving 10 miles to the supermarket, but when she heard about an organic vegetable delivery scheme run from a nearby farm by Friends of the Earth members she decided to give it a try. The weekly boxes of tasty, seasonal vegetables have been a great success. "I spend £20 a week less and have more time with my children," says Cathy. "I know they are eating safe, locally-grown fresh food. I want my family to have healthy food choices - to eat food free from pesticides and GM ingredients. Shopping in the supermarket didn't give me that choice."

In fact Cathy is not entirely right. Supermarkets stock two-thirds of the organic food sold in the UK, and they do so because customers are demanding a wide range of organic produce. "There's massive interest in organic products," says Sainsbury's Anthony Taylor, who works as an organic buyer. "The biggest volume of sales in groceries are tea, coffee and snacks, like our own brand and Duchy biscuits. Although cost is the biggest barrier to people buying organic lines, the demand for organic products is far outstripping supply. But this is changing."

Local support >

Supermarkets, always quick to follow the latest trends, are also starting to try and support local growers, but progress is still slow. And even when local foods are in stores they are often muddled up with shelves of other products and not given distinctive enough labelling. "We know from our customer panels that customers like to support local growers, the local community and buy local produce," says Melody Schuster, who also works at Tesco. The company stocks products from around 300 producers, more than 60 different types in peak season, which carry a special rosette and packaging which shows that they are locally grown. However, these are still routed through distribution centres and are often overpackaged.

However shoppers at the 18 flagship Rainbow Superstores of the Anglia Regional Co-operative Society, sited in Norfolk, Cambridgeshire and Suffolk, don't have to strain so hard to find local produce. Each store carries a two metre block of shelving devoted to local produce including beer, apple juices, preserves, chutneys and chocolate. The products are sourced by a local marketing organisation, Tastes of Anglia, which is hoping to add a range of chilled foods including locally-produced meat, sausages and yoghurt. A similar scheme is being trialed in Devon branches of Somerfield.

ASDA goes one better by converting corners at some of their vast car parks into a site for local produce sales on occasional weekends. During 1999 more than 200 farmers around the country had the chance to sell direct to ASDA shoppers. The first farmers' market was held at ASDA's Southampton superstore in May, but others followed at Brighton Hollingbury, Canterbury, Colne, Eastleigh, Kendal, Kilmarnock, Minworth, Morely, Newport, Norwich, Perth, Queensferry, Skelmersdale and Wolstanton. "It may be surprising to many to see a farmers' market in a supermarket, but this underlines ASDA's commitment as the leading retailer in support of British farming. And most importantly customers tell us that our 'British for Freshness' campaign is giving them real reason to buy British," said John Cleland Director of ASDA's produce, meat and poultry. Brave words from a supermarket giant, especially one that was sold the next month to the American retailer, Wal-Mart.

Many supermarkets are also introducing home delivery services, often after taking fax or e-mail orders. Home delivery has several benefits: it can reduce the amount of energy used by shoppers driving to and from the stores, and it also means that you do not have to carry your shopping any distance at all. Tesco already has an on-line service operating from 22 stores, but you can only use it if your postcode fits. "We find it is very popular in London because often people don't have cars, or they live in flats, and they don't want to carry their shopping home," explains Helen Bridget, who is Marketing Manager for Tesco On-Line. "It's mostly used by dual income professionals with kids, because both partners are working all day and they don't have time to shop; and because there are kids in the house shopping is a nightmare because of the physical size of things like packets of cereal and soft drinks."

Office convenience >>

Iceland, which banned products containing GMOs in its own brands long before the other supermarkets did the same, began a free home-delivery service for anyone spending £25 or more in March 1997, after trialing the concept in Scotland. "We identified that more than 65 per cent of our customers do not have access to a car during the day," said Barbara Crampton, a spokeswoman for Iceland. "It also means that you can do the shopping any time, you don't have to think, well that's frozen so I'll have to buy it last."

Summing up >

Old habits can be hard to break, and few people will be able to avoid supermarkets all the time. However what could be nicer than liberation from the weekly trawl around the superstore? Our Real Food Campaign should give shoppers inspiration to find the tastiest, most local, freshest food around. Some of this may be stocked in the supermarket, some may even be in the supermarket car park - but most is going to be a long way from the aisles. If you want to find real food stocked on supermarket shelves then ask to see it on sale. This is your chance to make a real difference to your health, farmers' livelihoods and the environment - and all you have to do is eat the best real food around.

What you can do >>
See six ways you can choose real food today, page 11.

Good label guide >>

Look out for labels like these when you're shopping

Organic Foods >

To be called organic, food must conform to stringent conditions. These certification symbols guarantee authenticity:

 Soil Association

 Organic Food Federation

 Biodynamic Agricultural Association

 Scottish Organic Producers' Association

 Organic Farmers and Growers' Association

 Irish Organic Farmers & Growers' Association

Fair trade >>

 Found on: a whole range of products from coffee to chocolate.

Guarantees: the producers of the product were paid a decent price, and that the product was produced at minimal cost to their environment.

GM-Free (food free from genetically modified ingredients) >>

 Remember, labels are only a first step. If all food was GM-free, we wouldn't need labels at all.

Supermarket quiz >>

To find out if the supermarket you shop at is making positive steps to support real food and the UK's farmers, try quizzing the store manager. Photocopy the quiz if it makes it easier to remember the questions.

GM foods >

>> When will your own brands be free from GM ingredients?

>> How easy will it be for me to recognise that they are GM-free? And whether all GM food will be labelled as such?

>> Will you make all the products on your shelves GM-free?

>> Will you introduce a GM aisle for GM products? This would save me having to check any labels.

Pesticides >

>> Please can you tell me about all the pesticides and artificial chemicals that have been used to grow your non-organic produce.

>> When are you going to tell shoppers that the Government recommends peeling fruit before it is fed to children? I would like to see this information clearly displayed throughout your fruit and vegetables section.

Staying in store ¶¶¶

Local food >

>> How much of your produce is grown locally?

>> Do you have any plans to stock more local produce to reduce the distance travelled by your products?

Organic products >

>> How many of the organic products on your shelves are grown and produced in the UK?

>> Will you stock more locally grown and produced organic products?

Waste >

>> What is your policy on reducing food waste and unnecessary packaging?

Antibiotics >

>> Do you have a policy for monitoring antibiotic residues in the meat and dairy produce you sell?

>> Do you have a policy of purchasing meat and dairy produce from flocks and herds that are not routinely treated with antibiotics?

Fair trade >

>> How are you improving the safety of workers at your overseas suppliers?

>> Do you pay a fair price for both UK and developing world farmers' products?

Chapter 9

After eight: summing up

For once it makes sense to be a fussy eater. The best way of ensuring you have the chance to eat real food is to make a fuss. Friends of the Earth knows this works - if the organisation had not spoken out there would still be secrecy about the amount of pesticides contaminating our drinking water.

Again and again Friends of the Earth has proved that people power really does work! Together with concerned shoppers the organisation has helped:

>> Encourage local education authorities to ban GM food from school canteens and catering establishments.

>> Persuaded the UK's top 23 restaurants - as listed in the *Good Food Guide 1999* - to support Friends of the Earth's call for a freeze on GM foods and crops.

>> Forced all major retailers and many food manufacturers to remove GM ingredients from their own-brand products with the help of consumer pressure.

But with your help we could do much more about making sure we all have a choice about eating real food. Friends of the Earth hopes that *The Real Food Book* has helped you understand what is going wrong - and right - with the UK's food system. Some of the early chapters make sorry reading. But there are also many inspiring and practical ways of supporting the farmers and producers who want to create the best possible, tastiest food for shoppers who care about the planet.

What you can do >>

>> Join Friends of the Earth and help create a safer, healthier, fairer world. Tel: 020 7490 1555.

>> Help Friends of the Earth get the Government to sign up to our Real Food Charter, see page 94.

Real Food Charter >>

To make sure that you have the choice to buy safe, healthy food Friends of the Earth and other organisations have drawn up a Real Food Charter and are calling on the Government to provide a good deal for farmers and to protect the countryside.

We want the Government to introduce:

>> A freeze on GM food and crops until they are proved safe, both for us and the environment.

>> A label for all GM foods - not just food that contains GM plants, but also foods that contain oils, starches, etc. from GM plants.

>> A tax on pesticides - to discourage excessive pesticide use and help support organic farmers.

>> A UK target of 30 per cent by 2010 for the percentage of land farmed organically, and a package of measures to support less intensive farming methods to produce real food.

>> Legal protection for wildlife habitats from damaging farming practices.

>> Legal protection for organic and non-organic farmers from genetic contamination of their crops.

>> Laws to make biotechnology companies strictly liable for all damage caused by GM food and crops.

 **Contacts**

Ask the supermarkets what they are doing to provide real food choices.

ASDA	0500 100 055	Somerfield	⎫	
Co-op	0800 317 827	Kwiksave	⎬	0117 935 6669
Iceland	01244 842 675	Gateway	⎭	
Marks & Spencer	020 7268 1234	Tesco		0800 505 555
Wm Morrison	01924 870 000	Waitrose		0800 188 884
Sainsbury's	0800 636 262			
Safeway	01622 712 987			

Ask your MP to tell the Government you want real food
How to contact your MP:
Tel: 020 7219 4272 • Web: www.locata.co.uk/commons/

Buying organic/delivery schemes

Baby Organix, Tel: 0800 393511 • Web: www.babyorganix.co.uk

Rachel's Dairy, Unit 63, Glanyrafon Industrial Estate, Aberystwyth, Wales SY23 3JQ • Tel: 01970 625805 • Web: www.rachelsdairy.co.uk

Riverford Organic Vegetables, Wash Barn, Buckfastleigh, Devon, TQ11 0LD
Tel: 01803 762720 • E-mail: riverford@zetnet.co.uk

The Soil Association, Bristol House, 40-56 Victoria St. , Bristol, BS1 6BY
Tel: 0117 9290661 • Fax: 0117 925 2504 • E-mail: info@soilassociation.org
Web: www.soilassociation.org

Vinceremos organic wines and beers by mail order, 261 Upper Town Street, Bramley, Leeds LS13 3JT • Tel: 0113 257 7545 • Fax: 0113 257 6906
E-mail: info@vinceremos.co.uk

Developing country concerns (patents, food security, GM crops)
Christian Aid, 35-41 Lower Marsh, Waterloo, London SE1 7RT • Tel: 020 7620 4444 • Fax: 020 7620 0719 • E-mail: info@christian-aid.org
Web: www.christian-aid.org.uk/main.htm

Effects of intensive farming on animals

Compassion in World Farming, Charles House, 5a Charles Street, Petersfield, Hampshire GU32 3EH
Tel: 01730 264208 • Fax: 01730 260791 • Web: www.ciwf.co.uk E-mail: info@ciwf.co.uk

Ethical food product information

Ethical Consumer Research Association, Unit 21, 41 Old Birley Street, Manchester, M15 5RF
Tel: 0161 226 2929 • Fax:0161 226 6277 • E-mail: ethicon@mcr1.poptel.org.uk, Web: www.ethicalconsumer.org

Fair trade and products which carry the fair trade logo

The Fairtrade Foundation, Suite 204, 16 Baldwin's Gardens, London EC1N 7RJ, UK • Tel: +44 (0)20 7405 5942 • Fax: +44 (0)20 7405 5943 • E-mail: mail@fairtrade.org.uk • Web: www.fairtrade.org.uk

Farmers' markets

For an updated list of farmers' markets please send an A5 SAE to the Soil Association, Bristol House, 40-56 Victoria St. , Bristol, BS1 6BY or visit its web site: www.soilassociation.org

General information on a range of food issues

Food Commission (UK) Ltd., 94 White Lion Street, London N1 9PF • Tel: 020 7837 2250 • Fax: 020 7837 1141 • E-mail: foodcomm@compuserve.com • Web: www.foodcomm.org.uk

Sustain, (formerly NFA and SAFE), 94 White Lion Street,N1 9PF • Tel: 020 7837 1228 • Fax: 020 7837 1141 • E-mail: sustain@charity.vfree.com
Web: http://users.charity.vfree.com/s/sustain

Genetic modification

Five Year Freeze Campaign, 94 White Lion Street, London, N1 9PF
Tel: 020 7837 0642 • Fax: 020 7837 1141 • E-mail: gealliance@dial.pipex.com
Web: www.dspace.dial.pipex.com/gealliance

Growing organic

Federation of City Farms and Community Gardens, The Green House, Hereford Street, Bedminster, Bristol BS3 4NA • Tel: 0117 923 1800
Growing Communities, The Old Fire Station, 61 Leswin Road, London N16 7NY

Web: www.btinternet.com/~grow.communities

Henry Doubleday Research Association, Ryton Organic Gardens, Ryton-on-Dunsmore, Coventry, West Midlands CV8 3LG • Tel: 01203 303517 Fax: 01203 639229 • E-mail: enquiry@hdra.org.uk Web: www.hdra.org.uk

Organic certification bodies

Biodynamic Agricultural Association, Painswick Inn Project, Gloucester Street, Stroud, Glos GL5 1QF • Tel: 01453 759501, 9am–1pm

Organic Farmers and Growers, 50 High Street, Soham, Ely, Cambridgeshire CB7 5HF • Tel: 01353 722398

Organic Food Federation, Tithe House, Peaseland Green, Elsing, East Dereham, Norfolk NR20 3DY • Tel: 01362 637314

The Soil Association, see above (buying organic)

Scottish Organic Producers' Association, Milton of Cambus, Doune, Perthshire FK16 6HG • Tel: 01786 841657

Irish Organic Farmers' and Growers' Association, Harbour Buildings, Harbour Road, Kilbeggan, Co. Westmeath, Ireland • Tel: (00353) 0506 32563

Pesticides in food

The Pesticides Trust, Eurolink Centre, 49 Effra Road, London, SW2 1BZ Tel: 020 7274 8895 • Fax: 020 7274 9084 • E-mail: pesttrust@gn.apc.org Web: www.gn.apc.org/pesticidestrust/

 **Books**

Luke Anderson, *Genetic Engineering, Food, and our Environment: A Brief Guide* (Green Books, 1999)

Joanna Blythman, *The Food We Eat* (Penguin, 1998)

Joanna Blythman, *The Food Our Children Eat* (Fourth Estate, 1999)

Lynda Brown, *The Shopper's Guide to Organic Food* (Fourth Estate, 1998)

Where to Buy Organic Food: A Directory of Farm Shops, Box Schemes and Retailers (Soil Association, 1998)

Glossary

Arable > farmland used for growing crops.

Biodiversity > the complete range of all living things in a given area.

Biotechnology > the science of genetic engineering.

Chemical residues > the remaining amounts of fertilisers, pesticides and antibiotics found in food.

Climate change > change to the world's climate caused by the build up of greenhouse gases in the atmosphere.

Conversion > the two or three years it takes for a farm to switch from conventional farming to farming which can be verified as organic by an independent certification body.

External costs > the costs of a practice which are not borne by the person or company doing it, but by wider society, such as the costs of purifying water contaminated by agro-chemicals.

Fertilisers > materials such as animal manures and artificial chemicals which aid plant growth.

Food miles > the distance an item of food travels from its source to the plate.

Genetic engineering > a science which allows scientists to create entirely new strains of plants and animals in the laboratory.

GMOs (or GM) > genetically modified organisms are produced when genes are transferred from one organism to another, thereby altering the DNA of the host organism. For example inserting an 'anti-freeze' gene, that enables a fish to survive in freezing water, into a tomato to make it frost-resistant.

Habitat > place where certain species of plants and animals live.

Herbicide > chemical weedkiller

Integrated crop management (ICM) > management and farming techniques to reduce the scale and impact of pest infestations.

Intensive farming > farming practices reliant on high inputs of chemicals and energy to increase yields.

Landfill site > a place where solid waste is disposed of by burying it, usually a hole in the ground.

Mixed farming > a traditional system of farming in which crops and livestock are raised on the same farm, allowing animal manure to be used as a crop fertiliser.

Monoculture > growing the same crop over a specific area again and again.

Nitrates > chemicals which are used in fertilisers to help plants grow. Nitrates can pollute rivers and underground water supplies.
Organic certification body > organisation which verifies whether a farm, crop or food product has been produced following organic principles.
Organic food > fruit, vegetables, food products and meat which is grown or raised without the use of artificial chemicals.
Organic farming > a type of farming which does not use artificial chemicals, such as fertilisers and pesticides.
Pesticide > a chemical used to kill pests, such as insects, weeds and fungi.
Pollution > any artificial contamination released into the environment which could cause harm to the environment or health.
Product lines > different types of products stocked by supermarkets.
Recycling > reprocessing waste materials so that they can be used again.
Super weeds > slang term for farmland plants which have gained resistance to some herbicides, thus requiring more, or stronger, herbicides to kill them.
Sustainable land use > practices which do not compromise the ability of future generations to use the land to meet their needs.
Terminator gene > a genetic engineering device to make the seeds of a crop sterile.
Vegetable boxes > bags or boxes of fresh, seasonal vegetables (and usually organic) supplied by a delivery service.

¶¶¶ Acronym buster

CAP >	Common Agriculture Policy		**GATT** >	General Agreement on Trade and Tariffs
DETR >	Department of Environment, Transport and the Regions		**NFU** >	National Farmers Union
			MAFF >	Ministry of Agriculture, Fisheries and Food
EC >	European Community			
EU >	European Union		**WTO** >	World Trade Organisation
FOE >	Friends of the Earth			

Index